D0806225

Imagining Nabokov

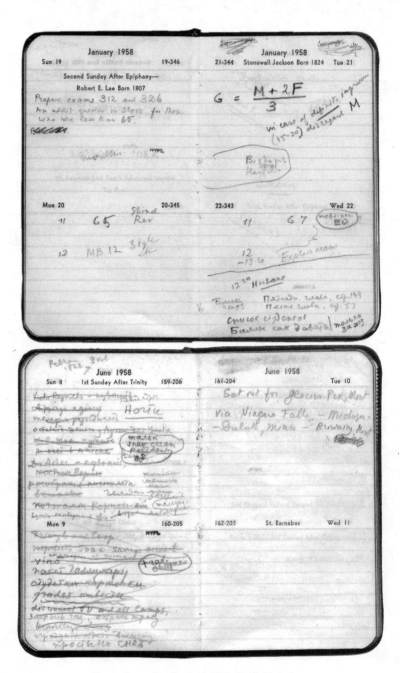

Pages from the diaries of Vladimir Nabokov

Imagining Nabokov

Russia Between Art and Politics

Nina L. Khrushcheva

YALE UNIVERSITY PRESS   NEW HAVEN & LONDON

Designed by Mary Valencia.
Set in Adobe Caslon type by Binghamton Valley Composition,
Binghamton, New York.

Printed in the United States of America.

Library of Congress Cataloging-in-Publication Data

Khrushcheva, Nina L., 1962–
Imagining Nabokov : Russia between art and politics / Nina L. Khrushcheva.
p. cm.
Includes bibliographical references and index.
ISBN 978-0-300-10886-6 (cloth : alk. paper)
1. Nabokov, Vladimir Vladimirovich, 1899–1977—Criticism and interpretation. I. Title.
PG3476.N3Z6987   2007
813'.54—dc22
2007027403

A catalogue record for this book is available from the Library of Congress and British Library.

The paper in this book meets the guidelines for permanence and durability of the Committee on Production Guidelines for Book Longevity of the Council on Library Resources.

10 9 8 7 6 5 4 3 2 1

To Andrei Sinyavsky (Abram Tertz)

I believe that one day a reappraiser will come and declare that, far from having been a frivolous firebird, I was a rigid moralist kicking sin, cuffing stupidity, ridiculing the vulgar and cruel—and assigning sovereign power to tenderness, talent, and pride.

—Vladimir Nabokov

Contents

Contents

Acknowledgments

My greatest debt of gratitude is owed to my mother, Julia Khrushcheva, who first made me think about literature's influence on politics, Nabokov, and pretty much everything else. In addition my special thanks go to Jonathan Brent, editorial director at Yale University Press, for accepting this book for the press and providing expert editorial advice. I am also especially grateful to Michael Wood for his exemplary way of reading Nabokov as well as for his intellectual generosity, kind encouragement, and invaluable comments following upon his patient reading of many versions of this manuscript. I would like to thank Caryl Emerson for first introducing me to the genius of Abram Tertz to whom this book is dedicated. I am grateful for her sympathetic, yet often critical reading of its various chapters. I am enormously indebted to

Kenneth Murphy for his ready assistance and advice in more instances than I can count. I also want to thank Alla Rachkov for her constant encouragement and support. My sincere thanks go to Yasen Nikolaevich Zasursky for providing me with an opportunity to teach a course on Nabokov at Moscow State University, and to my students there, to whose challenging questions I owe more than I can say. I am grateful to Douglas Greenfield and Nina Bouis for translating parts of this work from the Russian and to Michelle Linder and Katarzyna Kozanecka for helping with the preliminary editorial work. I am also grateful to Margaret Otzel for the meticulous production of the book and to Gavin Lewis for his excellent copyediting and his very helpful editorial suggestions. And last but not least I would like to thank the following people who were kind enough to share with me their own thoughts on Vladimir Nabokov, writing, art, language, politics, Russia and America, in addition to Caryl Emerson, Kenneth Murphy and Michael Wood: Anthony Anemone, Helen Atlas, Edward Baumeister, Boris Gasparov, Natalya Ivanova, David Jacobson, Adam Michnik, Serge Schmemann, Michael Scammell, and Tatyana Tolstaya.

Note on Transliteration
and Translations

Bibliographical references and Russian words cited in this book
follow a modified version of the Library of Congress system
of transliteration ("ya" instead of "ia," for example). Soft signs are
omitted from Russian words, and names are given in their standard
English form when one exists. Unless otherwise indicated, translations from the Russian are my own.

Abbreviations

PPP   "Pushkin, ili Pravda i pravdopodobie" ("*Pushkin, or Truth and Truthfulness*"), in *Sobranie sochinenii russkogo perioda*

RLSK   *The Real Life of Sebastian Knight*

SM   *Speak, Memory*

SO, A   *Strong Opinions*: Articles

SO, I   *Strong Opinions*: Interviews

VM   "The Visit to the Museum," in *The Stories of Vladimir Nabokov*

Chronology:
Works by Vladimir Sirin
and Vladimir Nabokov

SIRIN

1926   *Mashenka (Mary)*

1928   *Korol, Dama, Valet (King, Queen, Knave)*

1930   *Zashchita Luzhina (The Defense)*

1930   *Soglyadatai (The Eye)*

1931   *Otchayanie (Despair)*

1932   *Podvig (Glory)*

1932   *Kamera obskura*

1937   *Dar (The Gift)*

1938   *Laughter in the Dark* (in English)

1938   *Priglashenie na kazn (Invitation to a Beheading)*

NABOKOV

1940	*Lectures on Russian Literature*
1941	*The Real Life of Sebastian Knight*
1941–53	*Lectures on Literature*
1944	*Nikolai Gogol*
1947	*Bend Sinister*
1951	*Conclusive Evidence* (*Speak, Memory* 1966)
1954	*Drugie berega* (*Other Shores*)
1955	*Lolita*
1957	*Pnin*
1962	*Pale Fire*
1964	*Eugene Onegin*
1965	*Lolita* (in Russian)
1969	*Ada, or Ardor*
1972	*Transparent Things*
1973	*Strong Opinions*
1974	*Look at the Harlequins!*

Introduction:

Nabokov and Us

Art in its multiple efforts, in many searches for various paths,
charts up a path that all humanity will one day use.
—Victor Shklovsky, *Energiya zabluzhdeniya*

Vladimir Nabokov's journey from obscure Russian émigré writer to the author of American and world literary classics is essential for understanding Russia's past, its present, and its future. His lasting contribution to both Russian literature and Russian life is that—in his early prose and in his later English-language novels—he created characters of a kind dramatically different from those readers had come to expect in Russian literature: sufferers, revolutionaries, and madmen; men and women subservient to fate and in search of escape and salvation; people who readily excuse weakness (particularly their own) and see destruction and death as desirable ends.

A unique quality of Nabokov's characters is that, instead of exulting in the spirit of compassion and sympathy, rebellion and submission, that Russian literary characters—certainly those in Gogol and Dostoevsky—are supposed to indulge themselves in, they take responsibility for their own lives. They are often strong and positive in their outlook, in a manner almost unknown to the Russian literary sensibility. They make individual decisions, not only at the risk of seeming self-centered and arrogant like their predecessors Onegin and Pechorin,[1] but also with no qualms about doing so.

Before going further, I should warn readers that this is no traditional academic study of Nabokov's works, but is instead the fruit of my reflections on him over the past twenty some years. In this regard this book may seem intensely personal, yet despite its idiosyncratic character I hope it will spark conversation, if not in formal classroom discussions then at least around the dinner table, which is after all where so much of Russian family life takes place. My thinking about Nabokov has, at least in part, derived from my own lived experience as a representative of Russia's intelligentsia— somebody who studied Russian literature at Moscow State University, wept over the poetry of Anna Akhmatova,[2] and read Alexander Solzhenitsyn's *The Gulag Archipelago* (1973) in the quiet of the night during the stagnant Brezhnev years (1964–82). In this respect my reactions to Nabokov's work were similar to those of many Soviet readers. My reading of Nabokov, however, has also been informed by the notion that in a strange way, like him, I am considered a member of an aristocracy, albeit the Soviet one.

Vladimir Nabokov's family was of political significance in

Russia in the early 1900s. His father Vladimir Dmitrievich Nabokov was an intellectual and a member of Russia's aristocratic ruling class, serving in the Russian Provisional Government in 1917 before the Bolshevik Revolution. My own family was of Soviet political significance in the mid-1950s. From Joseph Stalin's death in 1953 to 1964 Nikita Khrushchev, my great-grandfather, headed the ruling class of the Communist *nomenklatura* as the party's General Secretary. The 1917 Bolshevik Revolution drove the Nabokovs out of the country depriving them of their aristocratic privileges. The 1964 plenary meeting of the Communist Politburo, masterminded by KGB hardliners, ousted Khrushchev for "voluntarism" (in essence, for his denunciation of Stalin's cult of personality, which Dmitri Nabokov, the writer's son, recently referred to as "one of the first cracks in the Communist monolith"),[3] giving the Kremlin's reins to his successor Leonid Brezhnev and sending Khrushchev into "dacha-exile" outside of Moscow. Despite the world of difference between these two "oustings" they qualify both families as part of a "deposed elite."

Vladimir Nabokov *was forced* first into European exile by the Bolsheviks in 1919 and then to America by the Nazis in the 1940s; Mikhail Gorbachev's perestroika of the late 1980s *presented* me with an opportunity to come to the United States in 1991. I first studied comparative literature at Princeton University, where I also learned a bit about international politics from George F. Kennan, who had so cogently analyzed Stalin and his regime, and from Jack F. Matlock, who supervised the ending of the Cold War as the last U.S. ambassador to the Soviet Union. I then went on to teach international affairs at the New School in New York.

Although I recognize that there exists a chasm between a political exile and a voluntary expatriate, I still feel myself a kindred spirit with Nabokov: from what our families had been in Russia's politics and society—the ruling class, we, Nabokov and I, both became thoroughly middle class in America. These similarities, I believe, provide the basis for a "dialogue" with the writer that is conducted not so much in English or Russian, as in the tones and according to the mores of modern Western democratic culture, the language of Western values shared by free individuals, the language that the new "Western" Russia, should it ever emerge, will need help and encouragement to speak.

While living in the United States, I have become more than Nabokov's reader, I've become something of a character of his, attempting to understand what it takes to be an individual, responsible for one's own actions, when no state ideology exists to provide your life with form and meaning. Nabokov and his works taught me "Westernization" first hand, i.e. how to be a single "I" instead of a member of the many "we" in that vast, undifferentiated, traditional Russian collective of the peasant commune, the proletarian mass, the Soviet people, the postcommunist *Rossiyane* (Russian nationals). It is the eternal *We* that Yevgeny Zamyatin depicted (1921) as a One State dystopian society, in which everyone is open to the gaze of everyone else in order to assure collective unity, a "we" in which individuals are of no value and free will is the cause of unhappiness. From Zamyatin's notion of a nation of "we"s—of sweeping revolutions and generalizations, which look with disdain at small deeds and bleed to save humanity but won't lift a finger to save a lone human being—Nabokov sought to liberate the thinking "I," with its requirement that each person achieve independence, particularly of conscience and reason. "I"s are the necessary contributors to the middle class, where an individual matters as much as the group and where the everyday life of a single person doesn't represent the common ills or grand victories of the state. This luxury of self-interest (and it is luxury for Russians, as we have known so little of it) was described by Adam Smith as a state of affairs in which "Every man, as long as he does not violate the laws of justice, is left perfectly free to pursue his own interest his own way, and to bring both his industry and capital into competition with those of any other man, or order of men."[4]

On the other hand, to the centuries-old Russian way of thinking, the individual is inferior to the community because the communal way of life—of brotherly equalizing love—forms the essence of Orthodox Christianity which occupies the core, and is at the origins of, Russia's national self-definition:

In Russian understanding Christianity is not just a faith the nation was baptized into. The Russian land itself, Russian nature was baptized and therefore assumed a God-favored and comforting aspect. In the people's belief

Christianity is not just a human but also a cosmic harmony.[5]

This "cosmic harmony" indeed defines the tradition of the peasant commune, described by the Slavophiles, the nineteenth-century advocates of Russian spiritual uniqueness, with the term *sobornost*, understood as the capacity for suffering, the universality of an all-encompassing Orthodox faith, as well as cultural unity (togetherness, harmony)—a perfect model of living exercised by the Russian *obshchina-mir* (the peasant commune; *mir* also means "world," "peace").

Celebrating this absolute faith, Orthodoxy represents to its adherents the higher spiritual mission of the people. Orthodoxy is considered superior to all Western brands of Christianity, which the Orthodox condemn for their materialism and pragmatism, especially in their approach to the human soul.[6] As Fyodor Dostoevsky, a fountainhead of Russia's philosophy of soulful suffering, once put it, Russia's spiritual mission ensures social harmony around the globe and guarantees that "the future of Europe belongs to Russia."[7]

Proud of its spiritual mission, Russia faulted the West[8] for believing, as later famously analyzed by Max Weber, that "God helps [only] those who help themselves"[9]—one only has to, as the saying goes, "pull oneself up by one's bootstraps." Many leading Slavophile thinkers despised the West for encouraging "people to organize their lives in a practical-rational manner," for championing the "inner *loneliness of the solitary individual*," and for "warning against all trust in the helpfulness of others and in friendship."[10]

For centuries Russians debated their special national path. Slavophiles, including nineteenth- and twentieth-century religious thinkers like Vladimir Solovyov and Nikolai Berdyaev, advocated communalism and antirationalism for the sake of obtaining divine justice and finding Russia's special road to God, while Westernizers from the nineteenth-century socialist democrat Vissarion Belinsky to later Marxists like Vladimir Lenin, insisted that Russians should revolutionize themselves, that is, behave and think as Europeans. However, history has proved that there has been a striking similarity between these two schools of thought—an overarching ideal of belonging to some higher harmonious order embodied in communal or communist form, in which only universal values, not individual rights, mattered. That is, ultimately both groups argued for the messianic destiny of the Russian nation—either in universal *sobornost* or in international communism.

This kind of grandiose thinking required that the individual be nationalized, i.e. that his membership in the commune of the devout Orthodox Christians or the builders of socialism should bring universal reason to lonely human existence. In 988 Christianity offered this kind of ideologically holistic faith, which in 1917 was duplicated by communism. In both instances it was fully embraced by the nation: "The new man did not want to stand out in any way from the masses; he labored not for himself

7

but for the common cause, in the name of the supreme goal: communism."[11]

In the words of the nineteenth-century Slavophile Alexei Khomyakov, Western "self-interest has no warranty in morality; material gain, a purely quantitative individual good, excludes the qualitative dimensions of life centered around service to the community."[12] Similarly, in 1920 Lenin addressed the Communist youth: "Our morality is entirely subordinate to the interests of the class struggle of the proletariat. . . . We say that morality is that which serves . . . the unification of all workers around the proletariat, which is creating a new society of Communists. . . . We do not believe in an eternal morality."[13]

This was in direct opposition to Adam Smith's pioneering liberal conviction that "proper" self-regard—self-interested behavior moderated by self-command and a sense of duty, as well as responsible adherence to social rules and obligations—can be socially beneficial.

Konstantin Aksakov, Khomyakov's Slavophile contemporary, opposed these "dispassionate"[14] Western social rules and obligations to Russian all-encompassing, passionate beliefs. "A commune," he wrote,

> is a union of the people, who have renounced their egoism, their individuality, and who express their common accord; this is an act of love, a noble Christian act. . . . A commune thus represents a moral choir, and just as in

a choir a voice is not lost, but follows the general pattern and is heard in the harmony of all voices: so in the commune the individual is not lost, but renounces his exclusiveness in favor of general accord—and there arises the noble phenomenon of the harmonious, joint existence of rational being (consciousness); there arises a brotherhood, a commune—a triumph of the human spirit.[15]

Now compare Aksakov's "moral choir" to the declaration of the author of the permanent revolution theory, Leon Trotsky, that "an *earthly paradise* was the raison d'être of the Communist movement,"[16] in which "the most egregious sin . . . is egoism or individualism, the desire to live for oneself as opposed to the common good."[17]

Essentially in any time period Russia has been torn between the *dream* of becoming Western (by adopting Christianity, Marxism, or American-style capitalism for that matter), and the *practical attempt* to become Western. Enamored of their nonmaterialistic soul (even dialectical materialism was highly nonmaterialistic in Soviet Russia) and a utopian state order (even such contemporary pragmatists as Anatoly Chubais, Russian privatization chief from 1991 to 1996, insisted Russian capitalism should be "built in just a few (*udarnykh*) shock years, meeting the norms of production which the rest of the world spent hundreds of years achieving"),[18] captivated by their own exploits of patient spiritual suffering or sweeping heroic deeds to save or shock the world commune, Russians preferred life's artistic representation to life itself.

Such practical triumphs as Peter the Great's Saint Petersburg, Lenin's 1917 Bolshevik Revolution, Stalin's Industrialization or Yeltsin's Privatization have been grandiose and arrogant creations of great "artists," who constructed their own exaggerated forms of politics, explaining this as the only way to move their inefficient yet enduring country forward. "Disorder saves Russia,"[19] has indeed been a consolation and an inspiration for generations of Russian revolutionaries. In all fairness, those "extreme" steps have indeed moved Russia towards Westernization; however, they have always come out of a typical Russian way of moving—a sweeping revolution of largely unhappy people instead of a calculated evolution of the generally content.

Even today in the twenty-first century Russians perceive themselves as the most unfairly treated nation on earth, one still requires some miraculous or heroic salvation by a mighty hero or "strong hand" ruler. This is not because Russian lives are particularly difficult (Nigeria, where women are stoned to death for adultery, is, after all, ranked first in global surveys of happiness in individual nations)[20] but because Russians continue to think that appearing as a unique soul, or an altogether misunderstood nation, is more satisfying than being a sated bourgeois in a comfortable country with no grand ideals to explore. From generation to generation the conscious, orderly, and patient accumulation of personal achievement and success has been in conflict with the Russian values of unlimited hospitality and humility, boundless passion, and universal love. Fate should take care of those who can't take care of themselves. Just compare these two wisdoms: the Russian saying, "He who gets up early receives alms from God," to its English equivalent, "Early to bed and early to rise, makes a man healthy, wealthy, and wise."

Here I would like to offer a slight digression and a warning to readers: discussing the West (by and large its American brand) this book at times will employ a somewhat typical, almost unavoidable Russian literary technique of large generalizations—for example, the use of the first person plural—we, our, us—when defining or describing cultural and historical concepts. Also it will be hard to avoid our traditional effort to encompass and explain the universe—that it is either *all* war or *all* peace as in Leo Tolstoy's *War and Peace* (1863–69). Possibly risking a reader's disapproval for scrappy, slapdash speculations, every so often I will take my chances and refer to various aspects of culture as if they represent *all* of Russia or *all* of America. Obviously, I am discussing not the raw realities of Russian or American life, but instead how they are viewed through the prism of the mind of my many Russian contemporaries. My analysis is not of some kind of unified monolithic societies of Russia and America, or some kind of amalgamated West, but of the cultural perceptions that Russians of today hold of those concepts. For both societies see each other through a looking glass of mythologies that represent (and sometimes substitute for) the living reality.

Anglo-Saxon-American mythology will be represented by Max Weber's study of *The Protestant Ethic and the Spirit of Capitalism,* first published in 1904–5. Weber's definition of an ethic of everyday behavior conducive to economic and social success is as valid for analyzing the transition of today's postsocialist societies as it was a hundred years ago for understanding their Western counterparts. His thesis that Protestantism (more accurately its Calvinist branches), by affirming the doctrine of predestination for each believer individually, created a new kind of man—rational, orderly, diligent, productive—thus remains useful in the context of my study. Here David Landes adds a helpful clarification:

This implicit reassurance [goodness as a plausible sign of election] was a powerful incentive to proper thoughts and behavior. And while hard belief in predestination did not last more than a generation or two . . . it was eventually converted into a secular code of behavior: hard work, honesty, seriousness, the thrifty use of money and time. . . .

Weber's "ideal type" of capitalist could be found [not] only among Calvinists and their later sectarian avatars. People of all faiths and no faith can grow up to be rational, diligent, orderly, productive, clean, and humorless. Nor do they have to be businessmen. One can show and profit by these qualities in all walks of life. . . . To people haunted by misery and hunger, that may add up to selfish indifference. But at bottom, no empowerment is so effective as self-empowerment.[21]

Russia, the United States' Cold War mirror image from the 1940s to the 1970s when Nabokov wrote his major works in English, in its turn will be looked at from the point of view of the favorite Russian maxim, usually attributed to Dostoevsky, "We are probably backward but we have a soul," which in conjunction with Abram Tertz's[22] observations on Russia's national philosophy and psychology provide for a reasonably accurate picture of our cultural mentality—inefficiency, patience, passionate emotionality, belief in miracles and material sacrifice, support for a "strong" (and often utopian) state, devotion to a *groznyi* (awesome, terrible)[23] ruler, as well as affinity with rebels and revolutionaries.

Nabokov, who vehemently disapproved of practically all of these amorphous qualities ("I am completely indifferent to the social aspect of . . . any . . . group activity" [*SO*, I#11, 133]), ultimately had to give up his native Russian tongue for English.[24] And although he cited a number of practical reasons for this linguistic switch, for example, the refusal of émigré journals to publish the fourth chapter of *Dar* (*The Gift*), his artistic reasons are clear: in English "I" is always a capital letter—not only does it never "renounce [its] exclusiveness in favor of general accord," it shamelessly starts most sentences.[25] Nabokov loved the prim and proper "I," which—unlike the tiny, derided Russian "я" (*ya*)—is anything but "the last letter of an alphabet."[26] Michael Scammell, who once translated Nabokov's *The Gift* and *The Defense* with the author's collaboration, is still amazed about how "Western" Nabokov's Russian was: "On a syntactical level, Nabokov turned out to be surprisingly easy to translate. His Russian was saturated with echoes of French and English, and his sentence structure was very Latinate."[27]

The English "I" allowed Nabokov to avoid countless impersonal Russian constructions such as *mne kholodno*—it's cold *to me, mne khochetsya*—it is desirable *to me, mne stydno*—it's a shame *to me, mne grustno*—it's sad *to me, mne strashno*—it's fearful *to me.* These grammatical forms reflect a culture in which people refuse responsibility for their feelings, sensations, and emotional experiences. It seems that it is not "I," who is the master of my feelings but someone else, invisibly manipulating my fortune and misfortune. The Russian "ya" always sees itself as an *object* of action, not its subject, leaving it to the collective "we" to define the world. In English, however, "I" is capable not only of making its own destiny, but of removing those obstacles that inconveniently get in the way.

Nabokov not only accepted a Western way of relating to the world, he made it his own, considering it crucial for survival in his adopted American homeland. Not at all religious, he was nevertheless completely sympathetic to that "devout Puritan, who is basically concerned only with himself and thinking only of his own salvation."[28] It was not for nothing that Nabokov called himself "an English child" (*SO*, I#6, 81), expressly stressing on another occasion that "I learned to read English before I could read Russian" and that "The kind of Russian family to which I belonged—a kind now extinct—had, among other virtues, a traditional leaning toward the comfortable products of Anglo-Saxon civilization" (*SM*, 57).

Nabokov's early postemigration Russian-language works (1920–40) were an exercise in testing out Western literary and cultural models. In *Despair, King, Queen, Knave, Mary,* and *Glory* he attempts to break from the vague, amorphous, and inflated digressions and metaphors of "circular" Russian literature, known for its dead ends and no-ends.[29] The setting of *King, Queen, Knave,* for example, recalls the bourgeois realism of Theodore Dreiser's *An American Tragedy* (1925), which, along with the work of Erich Maria Remarque, and others, represented for Russians the canon of Western prose style in the 1920s.

Some critics may disagree with the comparison to Dreiser, on the grounds that Nabokov would never have imitated those he did not admire (or even those he did). They could cite as evidence Nabokov's statement that "Ever since the days when such formidable mediocrities as Galsworthy, Dreiser, a person called Tagore, another called Maxim Gorky, a third called Romain Rolland, used to be accepted as geniuses, I have been perplexed and amused by fabricated notions about so-called 'great books'" (*SO*, I#5, 57).

However, I believe that Nabokov purposely parodied certain Western literary types to prove that Russian culture could sustain its own "individual-centered" literature. Instead of stories about the overwhelming suffering of Akaky Akakievich Bashmachkin, from whose *Overcoat* "we all came,"[30] Nabokov offered the well-to-do Herman (*Despair*) who commits a murder pursuing his carefree, selfish life. By using a prototypical Western anti-hero, Nabokov wills into creation a new type of Russian character, epitomized by Fyodor Godunov-Cherdyntsev in *The Gift*. Although "polozhitelnyi" (positive), this egoistic, self-absorbed character opened up new territory for Russian literature.

Despite these innovations, however, the Russian language with its impersonal constructions and lengthy metaphors still remained in Nabokov's way, preventing the emergence of a new, efficient, and self-centered character, a practical "Weberian" individual, a "dispassionate, 'self-made man,'"[31] free from the unnecessary burdens of emotional digressions, romantic sorrows, and first persons plural. Only after abandoning this burdensome and diffident Russian tongue, as he did in *Lolita, Pnin*, and *Ada, or Ardor,* was Nabokov able to realize his goal of remaking Russia through a new medium—the rational, linear, sensible, and sequential language of capitalist England and America. Yet, as my book will discuss, those very novels he considered unequivocally American betray him as a truly Russian writer.

One of Nabokov's characters, Martin Edelweiss in *Glory,* similarly discovers his absolute *Russianness* when he emigrates to Europe. Martin's secret return to his homeland, an irrational exploit from the standpoint of Western pragmatism (Martin's

British friend Darwin muses, "[W]ould it not be simpler to obtain a regular Soviet visa?" [*Glory*, 199]), perfectly reflects the emotional and uncalculating Russian character. Abram Tertz defined this type of character best:

> Our national characteristics—a natural inclination to anarchy (which, seen from outside, is commonly mistaken for barbarous or immature behavior), fluidity, amorphousness, readiness to adopt any mold ("come and rule over us"), our gift—or vice—of thinking and living artistically, combined with an inability to manage the very serious practical side of daily life: "Why bother? Who cares?" we ask. In this sense Russia offers a most favorable soil for the experiments and fantasies of the artist, though his lot as a human being is sometimes very terrible indeed.[32]

Nabokov serves as a model for the new Russia—in its attempts to finally create a favorable soil not just for the artist but also for the human being. He proved to be the first to foresee his country's transformation into one that should find its place in an open, individualistic, yet global world: "I cannot predict anything though I certainly hope that under the influence of the West, and especially under that of America, the Soviet police state will gradually wither away" (*SO*, I#4, 50).

Like all Russians, Nabokov admired Alexander Pushkin and agreed with his idea of the artist—"You are a czar, exist alone."[33]

"Today, more than ever, a poet should be as free, solitary and lonely as Pushkin wanted a hundred years ago," he once wrote (PPP, 550). However, in his work the writer disputed another demand of Pushkin, that the poet should serve as a prophet, "going over land and sea, / Burn human hearts with your Word" (*The Prophet*, 1826).[34] Nabokov insisted that "for an artist one consolation is that in a free country he is not actually forced to produce guidebooks" (*LORL*, 2).

A creator of elegant chess problems, Nabokov explained that he wrote his books only to please himself by overcoming the difficulties of composition: "I have no social purpose, no moral message; I've no general ideas to exploit, I just like composing riddles with elegant solutions" (*SO*, I#2, 16). Yet through his novels he was composing a new, different—individualistic and noncommunal—"Western" Russia with new elegant solutions. His books were banned in the Soviet Union for decades as a result.

Before the fall of the Berlin Wall in 1989 and the subsequent 1991 collapse of the Soviet Union, Russian readers overwhelmingly honored Nabokov as an emigrant writer but always from an intellectual distance. Most found it difficult to relate to him emotionally as a truly Russian author, "who is not only 'almost entirely divorced from current Russian problems, but whose place is outside of any direct influence of the Russian classical literature.'"[35] The brilliance of his style was often seen as a façade that covered up emptiness (that is, the lack of a moral message for the common good). His gliding images seemed nothing more than a smoke screen seen in a mirror.

And yet, in the last dozen years a change has been occurring, slowly: Nabokov's smoke screens and mirror reflections have come to be appreciated as genuine "okna na zapad" (windows onto the West). The Potemkin façades have been gradually evolving into bona fide buildings.

Following his own sobering experience of Westernization Nabokov defined the rules of existence for postcommunist Russians in a new time of banal rationalism, personal competition, and individual comfort. He explained how going over to a capitalist way of thinking—understood as growing pragmatism, efficiency, personal success and a sense of individual responsibility—should change the benevolent, slothful, and impractical Oblomov-like[36] Russian attitude to life.

Despite himself—"It is not my custom to display my political credo"[37]—Vladimir Nabokov became a writer indispensable to understanding the political and social developments of contemporary Russia. He successfully "rewrote" Russian literature for us. He reinvented Russia's dramatic characters, adjusting them to the new Western realities of what may be a less emotional, but surely a more sensible life. He proved wrong a critical claim that his writing presented only a "novelty of narrative technique and not of a novel perception of life."[38]

The "American" Nabokov of the second half of the twentieth century is the most important cultural and literary phenomenon for Russia in the first half of the twenty-first. He is our textbook, and our road map for today's transitional period from a closed and communal terrain to its Western alternative, one open and competitive. How to survive and succeed in this Western world, which Russia always deemed linear, cold, and calculating: this is what the art of Vladimir Nabokov teaches us.

Prologue:

Nabokov's Russian Return . . .
and Retreat

It was a matter of fierce pride for any Bolshevik: Russians read more than any other people on earth. In the postcommunist era, this fact bewildered countless Western economists and management consultants, who could not help but note that hypothetical and literary concepts have a far greater hold on Russia's people than practical ones.

These Westerners often dubbed Russian culture as "high-context,"[1] meaning that the way Russians communicate is loaded with hidden content—background information shared only by the "insiders" (*svoi, nashi*) versus the "others" (*chuzhie*). In negotiating a business contract, as a high-context culture Russia favors a "circular way of thinking," they complained. For example, "circular Russian thinkers" tend to approach the deal as a whole—panoramically, artistically—and want to solve all the problems all at once. On the contrary, low-context cultures, such as Anglo-Saxon-American ones, do not rely on hidden knowledge, provide factual explanation understandable to all, and use "linear thinking" in order to try to resolve problems one at a time—evolutionarily.

One result of these "cultural disparities" is that the ideas of capitalism and democracy in Russia scarcely resemble any Western conception of those structures. Moscow's bookstores, however, are a bibliophile's dream.

My Russian heart warmed to see that despite today's oligarchs and robber barons, our "Wild West" or "Kremlin" capitalism, Internet access, trendy restaurants, pubs, and the multiple jobs people keep just to make ends meet in these frenzied times of democratization, Russians still read books—and constantly. My Americanized "rational" mind, however, longs to find a practical way for Russia's passion for reading, and its belief in the writer as prophet, to be made more generally beneficial. Here, after all, in the "stagnant" 1970s Solzhenitsyn and the dissident writers were more important than Brezhnev and the politicians.

RETURN . . .

In the spring of 2001, full of nearly messianic intentions, I took a semester off from my research on Russia's political and economic transition to do a few months of teaching at Moscow State University, where I was to give a course on Vladimir Nabokov,

"Nabokov and Us." Of course, I saw myself in many ways walking in Nabokov's footsteps: the long years I had spent in Princeton and New York had turned a somewhat highbrow, otherworldly Russian intellectual into a practical Westerner.

So in returning to Moscow I felt I had something to reveal to my fellow Russians: to become liberal and free, Russia must put its best traditions of reading to "practical" use. We should switch to reading Nabokov rather than simply try to make sense of IMF briefs—official documents, after all, have never been a Russian forte—for Nabokov may provide a better road map of the way forward than the uncertain successes of faraway Indonesia or Brazil. Nabokov was able to remain Russian, consistently and un-ambiguously, yet be modern and Western at the same time. He was a model of international success, for he kept his soul without having to remain backward in order to do so.

Like all missionaries, I was humbled to discover (with satis-faction rather than disappointment) that I was late with my "good news." Nabokov, who stoically accepted (or at least claimed sto-ically to accept) that he would have very few readers in his social-ist homeland—indeed, he imagined his audience in Russia as a "room filled with people, wearing his own mask" (*SO*, I#2, 18)—would have been extremely delighted at his reception in his homeland half a century later: many in his country, particularly those with youthful faces, were wearing his mask.

Indeed, what I discovered was that the thrusting modern Russians were reading Nabokov into everything. In response to a carved bust of President Putin, Russians quoted Nabokov: "Portraits of the head of the government should not exceed a postage stamp in size" (*SO*, I#3, 35). Those who still stubbornly disregarded material comfort recalled his phrase about the "nuisance of private ownership" (ibid., I#13, 149); those who insisted on individualistic values followed him in being "an indivisible monist" (ibid., I#6, 85). Nabokov was translated, retranslated, and republished. During my browsing at the bookstore I even stumbled upon a *Nabokov Reader*, a guidebook for schoolteachers on how and why every adolescent in Russia should read Nabokov.

Expecting just a few fanatic students in my class at Moscow State, I instead walked into the room to find that with each session the number of people wearing Nabokov's mask doubled or tripled. The first week I had six students, the next, twelve, then eighteen . . . They were deft and determined—they recited passages from *Lolita* and *Speak, Memory* by heart in both English and Russian; they didn't skip classes or make excuses as we had done in my own time. Instead of weeping with pity over Anna Akhmatova's *Requiem*, or helplessly whispering about Alexander Solzhenitsyn's *Gulag Archipelago* in some kitchen, these post-postcommunist new-century kids were able to put literature to "practical" use. They told me that they found the nineteenth-century writers too dramatic, too pathetic; and those of the twentieth century too critical, unhappy, and dissident. Postcommunist literature is too trashy. But Nabokov is just right!

"Pushkin has been everything for you, Nabokov is 'our

Pushkin'"—and I detected a tinge of disdain for Russia's hardened literary traditions. "He managed"—their faces brighten with admiration—"to remain 'high' literature and nonetheless be concise and precise, a great stylist with original themes and a brave, strong, and victorious individual as hero." "My favorite creatures, my resplendent characters—in *The Gift*, in *Invitation to a Beheading*, in *Ada*, in *Glory*, et cetera—are victors in the long run" (*SO*, I#19, 193), they passionately quote. "We," they say with pride in themselves, "are that 'et cetera.' Nabokov is a literary manual for our everyday life on the road from the impractical Russian intellectual to the efficient, pragmatic, Western individual." "Something like Pnin, but better," one girl added resolutely.

"Why do you need me, then, why do you come to this class?" I asked the now thirty students in the room. They said they needed somebody who had already gone the way Nabokov and his characters had gone—to make sure it was doable, to live through the experience of his books.

My book, *Imagining Nabokov*, was written because of that novel generation of Nabokovian Russians. I dedicate it to Andrei Sinyavsky (Abram Tertz) who once courageously strolled with Pushkin so we could freely and fearlessly imagine Nabokov today.

. . . AND RETREAT

In 2006, the book almost finished, I went back to Russia, this time to Saint Petersburg, Nabokov's native city, to discuss my findings in the museum dedicated to him, which now occupies a few rooms on the first floor in the old Nabokov mansion on Bolshaya Morskaya Street. In an oak-paneled library that hosted a rather scarce but nicely displayed exhibit of Nabokov-related materials— books, sketches, and butterflies—I talked about Nabokov's Russian return yet again.

But this time around I had truly come late with my "good news." Sixteen years after the collapse of the Soviet Union, the last six of which President Vladimir Putin had spent reestablishing the centralized power of the Kremlin by diminishing the power of the institutions of civil society, most Russians no longer regard their country's openness to the rest of Europe as a sign that they have, at long last, united with Western civilization. The nine years during which Yeltsin was creating a new democratic Russia—one unpredictable, wayward, but full of promise—are now seen as a source of insecurity, because his American-style democratization of the 1990s failed to instantly bring *"idealnyi"* (ideal) capitalism. Moreover, with NATO and the European Union expanding right up to the country's borders; with America seen as wanting to weaken Russia even more, loosening its grip on the "near abroad" by supporting democratizing "color" revolutions in countries like Georgia in 2003 and Ukraine in 2004, anti-western sentiments are on the rise.

In April 2005 in his annual State of the Nation address President Putin described the collapse of the Soviet Union as "the greatest geopolitical catastrophe" of the twentieth century, "a genuine tragedy" for the Russian people. Despite his declaration that

Russia should continue to pursue free and democratic development, he stressed the necessity to "protect Russia's national identity, its own values, hold on to its heritage, find its own path to democracy."[2]

In this way Putin sought to put an end to the epochal changes Russia had gone through since Gorbachev's reforms, which not only liberated the country from the straitjacket of Marxism-Leninism, but also released the national aspirations of people who had been locked in the empire for centuries, allowing them to experience freedom of the press, of choice, of their way of life. Despite these changes, the Russians, true to their "circular" cultural development, seemed less eager to move forward towards their democratic future than to go back to the old ways of the country's autocratic past—to the grand pronouncements of Russia as a unique great nation, destined to rule the world.

The nation has repeatedly boasted of its various *special* forms of greatness. First it was the holy Russian soul, so superior to Western practicality. In the fifteenth century, after the collapse of the Byzantine Empire, Moscow was declared a "Third Rome," the savior of spiritual Christianity. The seventeenth century united this spiritual mission with imperial expansion, which eventually encompassed a landmass spanning eleven time zones. In the early twentieth century, the imperial and spiritual missions became one, as Russia became the bastion of world communism. In the twenty-first century high oil and gas prices have helped Russia's president to rebuild and maintain the image of a "strong state," or as Putin put it himself, "natural resources offered the key to Russia 'regaining its former might.'"[3] Indeed, "Russia's natural resource potential defines its *special* place among industrialized countries."[4] So mankind would once again tremble with respect and fear, this time not of the prospect of a Red Army invasion, but of a Gazprom cutoff of gas.[5]

Russian cultural instincts, in which communal ideas and a "great state" agenda remain more valued than individualist principles, helped determine the success of Putin's policies. In his quest for a "special" Russian democracy Putin is supported by 75 percent of the population.[6] He is liked by the old, who grew up in a communist welfare state and want its safety net back, however confining—with no individual choices to be made, and more predictable, if more miserable, social and economic conditions. The young, too, those with good "Western"-type jobs in banks or PR firms, have their doubts about the value of democracy in the Russian case and now seem to believe in the superiority of Russia's state-directed oil-driven market economy over a free-market version. Russians in general, with their ingrained idea of the country's uniqueness and special messianic status, don't want to be citizens of a *weak and insignificant Russia* that has been losing its greatness under the pressure of Western (particularly American) cultural and economic influences.[7] Reassured by their good jobs and access to consumer products, most Russians today welcome "Putinism" (an all-inclusive hybrid—Brezhnevism,[8] communism, KGB-ism, market-ism with some remaining freedoms) as a comforting "golden mean" between radical reforms and strong-arm rule.

In this political environment an emigrant Nabokov, whose books the Russians were so eager to discover only six years ago, is no longer treated as a pioneer who defines modern Russia for its citizens. In fact, I've heard complaints that he shouldn't be competing with other national writers and especially with Pushkin (reference to Nabokov's "arrogant" commentary to *Eugene Onegin*)—the *Solntse russkoi poezii* (sun of Russian poetry), the author of *Onegin* and *The Bronze Horseman*,[9] classics every Russian knows by heart.

Nabokov is just that—the distant creator of lapidary prose that's as beautiful and cold as the shimmering halls of the Snow Queen's castle, the author of American masterpieces, entomological classifications, and skillful chess puzzles. His *Invitation to a Beheading*, that exquisite, blood-chilling oxymoron, cannot be possibly compared to the undemanding and soothing "Bochka po moryu plyvet" ("A barrel swims through a restless sea").[10] He is too aloof and too formal; too inaccessible, unsociable, nonconformist, intellectual: "I do not write for groups, nor approve of group therapy. . . . I write for myself in multiplicate, a not unfamiliar phenomenon on the horizons of shimmering deserts" (*SO*, I#8, 114), or "I loathe popular pulp, I loathe go-go gangs, I loathe jungle music, I loathe science fiction with its gals and goons. . . . I especially loathe vulgar movies. . . . I mock popular trash" (ibid., I#9, 117). Nabokov doesn't mix well with the masses.

Russians have played with being his characters and have given them up—too difficult: they are too self-controlled, too self-sufficient. Instead of taking cues from Nabokov on how to suppress our ancient penchant for phrases that stretch for pages; how to overcome our weakness for circular, ring compositions, in literature, geography, and architecture,[11] and for approaching things panoramically, stretching them throughout an endless imperial plain with its eleven time zones; how to master our overwhelming desire to say everything at once and to write not a novel but a gospel, and to express ourselves clearly and concisely, we have wasted his lessons by turning them either into advertising kitsch or mindless soaps.

For example, today Pushkin's greatness is reduced to his portrait in the windows of drugstores and supermarkets and to posters hanging over highways with simple slogans like "Honor" against a background of dueling pistols,[12] or "Muse" against something dull and indistinct.

Meanwhile, other Russian and Soviet literary classics— Fyodor Dostoevsky's *The Idiot*, Mikhail Bulgakov's *Master and Margarita*, Alexander Solzhenitsyn's *First Circle* (1968), and Boris Pasternak's *Doctor Zhivago* (1956)—have recently been made into television miniseries.[13] Responding to a national desire to avoid the extremes of Soviet socialism or postcommunist capitalism, Russian culture has started to turn historic, literary, and human tragedies into entertaining simulations of greatness, now devoid of real suffering and threats. In a badly imitated Hollywood style, troubles are dispelled in hour-long, easily digestible episodes, allowing viewers to relive former grandeur and terror through the safe medium of television screens.

Hardly a worthy Nabokovian project. But eager to reclaim the country's significance and self-image, lost with the Cold War defeat, by any means possible, Russia has all but given Nabokov up along with his characters and his master classes, as it has given up the democratic reforms, growing too impatient to see them through.

The prominent nineteenth-century Russian philosopher Pyotr Chaadaev noted that "the most important feature of our [Russian] historic makeup is the absence of free initiative in our social development."[14] In fact, every important political idea that has shaped Russia came from abroad, while the nation itself was a historical tabula rasa, susceptible to all influences, with no beliefs of its own. A specific character of Russian culture was that it was "brought from elsewhere, and imitative. Russians take on only absolutely ready ideas, want them completed quickly, and thus do not inherit experiences related to making these ideas work in reality. Therefore, we grow but do not mature; move forward not in a linear but a curving, circular fashion, with no goal in front of us. We are an exception among nations. We exist in order to give a great lesson to the world."[15]

The 1917 Bolshevik Revolution was one of those ready-made ideas attempting to rationalize the Russian mystical land by applying Karl Marx's dialectical materialism to a country that moves forward not through sequential steps, but by emotional and physical explosions—in a word, revolutions. Similarly, post-1991 American-style capitalism was made to happen "in just a few shock years," which in turn brought not the desired results of capitalism and democracy but instead disillusion and mistrust for large sectors of the Russian public.

However, when democracy doesn't work properly, "bad" government is only partly to blame as real capitalism and democracy, besides needing responsible leadership, also require responsible citizens. But since 1991 the nation has been increasingly lost without a large guiding ideology, one that it can use to define itself as a state—"the country, deprived of high ideals, in just a few decades has rotted to the ground."[16]

In 2006 Saint Petersburg, I discovered that I was writing my book as an *encouragement* for Russians not to give up: Russia shouldn't revert from the promise to change from the communal "we" to the free individual "I" that it so bravely made nearly two decades ago. Besides, our latest Westernization attempt should do better than ever before, as now for the first time Russian literature can boast not only a formulation of the "accursed" Russian questions, *Who Is to Blame?* and *What is to be Done?*,[17] or a condemnation of the Soviet system such as *The Gulag Archipelago*, but a model to follow in the Nabokovian character, who understands how to survive the trials and tribulations of a transitional period.

That was my message to some seventy plus people, gathered in the library of the Nabokov Museum. This time around just a few young faces were hovering at the back of the room. They agreed that Nabokov is great literature—Russians rule! But do we really need to continue to be obsessed by his social and political importance, they asked. "Things are great, the country is doing well—strong and powerful again," a young man added resolutely. He believed that although capitalism and democracy are fine ideas, Putin's version of them was better than Nabokov's—state stability merged with state capitalism, instead of the real democratic/ free-market notion that there is no one but yourself, a solitary individual, to blame if things don't work out.

There were two other groups in the museum audience, somewhat older former Soviets who, although very familiar with the Russian tradition of reading literature as politics, also had no intention of allowing me to interpret Nabokov the way I was doing, let alone of reading him that way themselves.

One group was puzzled to see an offspring of the *nomenklatura* there at all—I should have been riding a limo to a party, not writing books on Russian political exiles. In the *nomenklatura* hierarchy after Nikita Khrushchev was ousted in 1964, he no longer had a place. But the public, unaware of these political intricacies, still considered me Kremlin kin.

The important question for the audience was not what I had to say about Nabokov's democracy and Russia's Westernization but about Khrushchev. A woman in her sixties insisted that it would have made perfect sense if her daughter, encouraged by Mikhail Gorbachev's perestroika, had decided to leave Russia to make a better future for herself in the United States, but why would I? My position as the member of the political elite should have provided me with all sorts of opportunities that I might never get on my own in America.

She wanted to know why I would want to stop being a Khrushchev and leave Moscow first for graduate school in Princeton and then for New York to become me—to teach, write, lecture. . . . As a people relatively new to democracy, Russians seem to still believe in "czars," not human beings. In this hierarchy my life has little value apart from that of my name. (This of course happens to many descendants of historical figures: under the heavy weight of a famous name, for the world at large they forever remain just an offspring.) By deciding to exist as an individual on my own I seemed to have ruined their autocratic dream that life up above (*naverkhu*), with the czars, is better.

The other group was enraged that an offspring of the Soviet elite dared to touch the holy of holies—Nabokov, the greatest exile, who despised the communists for ruining his country, his family, his city, and his life. How dare those Moscow Kremlin mugs study, think, speak about *our* Nabokov, kindred spirit to all of us, who hate the Soviet *nomenklatura* as much as he did? Moreover, how dare anyone read politics into Nabokov who, providing his readers with an escape from politics, proudly declared: "I am all for the ivory tower" (*SO*, I#3, 37)? Besides, Nabokov had made a few unpleasant remarks about Khrushchev, both in fiction and in essays.[18] Thinking in a simplistic communism-and-commune-instilled ideological zero-sum paradigm, they expected me to hate Nabokov in return, not to love him.

Another woman in her sixties, a lifelong Nabokov fan and a docent at the museum, was particularly indignant: How could you possibly understand our great treasure—a bastion of anticommunist escapism, a citadel of pure aesthetics free from the oppressive socially purposeful Soviet literature? And on top of it, who are you to teach us about Russia while living in America, she asked. Later I was told she had always wanted to emigrate to the United States, but, first, the communist monolith got in the way, and when perestroika opened up the borders she was too old to learn to adjust to a new country. Thirty years her junior, I had stolen her dream.

"This *nomenklatura*"—her voice trembled with a mixture of envy and disgust—"they took up the best spots and positions." As if, by autocratic fiat, in a free world my Kremlin origins somehow had handed me my individual life and forever protected me from difficulties, disillusions, and disappointments.

Whatever you have, she said, has been usurped and is not deserved. Nabokov *had* to emigrate because of you (she meant the Reds), you (she meant me) didn't. But I didn't emigrate—in a free world you don't have to. Like millions of free other people from hundreds of other free countries I, not Khrushchev, came to America to study, not to stay. And then stayed on because of my life, not Khrushchev's. But it was no use explaining that one can't "take up the best positions" while writing books. And teaching at the New School is not an invitation to attend the Hôtel de Crillon annual Bals de Debutantes in Paris, *only* because you are an offspring of Silvio Berlusconi, Danielle Steel, Leo Tolstoy, or Mikhail Gorbachev, for that matter.

So there I was, a traitor on all fronts.

ONE

Imagining Nabokov

The real writer should ignore all readers but one, that of the future,
who in his turn is merely the author reflected in time.

—Vladimir Nabokov, *The Gift*

MAKING HIS ACQUAINTANCE

The world is right not to pardon those who converse with geniuses, those who deem themselves worthy of great encounters, acquaintances, attention. Who do they think they are, anyway?

Abram Tertz was snubbed by the Russian artistic intelligentsia for his *Strolls with Pushkin*. Who does he think he is to frivolously write about "Pushkin [who] ran into great poetry on thin erotic legs and created a commotion"?[1] To avoid angering my own readers, I justify my familiarity with Nabokov by offering the writer's words in my defense: "Give me the creative reader: this is a tale for him" (*LORL*, 54).

Nabokov is exquisite and insufferable all at once. You can't explain him; you can only create him, each by oneself, for oneself.

"I write for myself in multiplicate" (*SO*, I#8, 114), my hero once said about his audience. So I read him for myself in the plural, which is why I'm writing this book: for everyone who—like Nabokov himself—values living in a free society; for everyone who—like my Moscow University students—wants to better learn the intricacies of this life.

At the risk of resembling Kinbote, *Pale Fire*'s eccentric commentator of John Shade's poem and exiled ruler of faraway Zembla—"for better or worse, it is the commentator who has the last word" (*PF*, 28–29)—in my own commentary I will take Nabokov at his word that literature must be read no less creatively than it is written.

Being brought up in Russia, where literature and life often mix into a single cultural reality, I am that reader, who would always imagine Nabokov and his heroes as something far more tangible than just a writer and his books. "The Word for us is such a substantial entity (spiritually) that it comes to resemble a physical force,"[2] Tertz once wrote.

Obviously, the Russians are not the only ones who imaginatively perceive literature and its heroes as real. Though Americans en masse seem to lack this habit of reading, it is a trait of other countries on the European continent. So it is not the originality of Russia's relationship to literature that is striking in its influence on the public mind and everyday life, it is its radicalism.

This radicalism derives from the fact that in a society of "we" the man has the habit of representing the masses or the class, which affects his own idea of himself and the world around him. This man (woman, person) is never solitary, doesn't act alone, and has a constant sense of a collective behind him. Reflecting this kind of culture (and simultaneously creating it) each major character in Russian literature is written as a "type," that is as a general representative of a certain group of the Russian people. Therefore, flesh-and-blood individuals, regarding themselves as general types, tend to relate to Russian literary texts as if these texts were describing their regular lives. In Russia you can often hear the following only half-joking admission, "We live in Gogol, . . . Dostoevsky, . . . Bulgakov. . . ."

Some critics also explain this radicalism by the absolute, all-consuming spirituality of Russia's Orthodox culture, where suffering, salvation, and enchantment are the main constants: "Our Russian feeling for miracles, icons, relics and ritual is fed by sensitivity to the life-giving Holy Spirit so intense that it approaches the reception of magical impulses. The Holy Spirit permeates the world, and . . . invites the whole of creation and all earthly flesh to partake in the bounties of the spirit."[3]

Undeniably, the work of art is the most complete expression of this enchanted spirit—its culmination. But morsels of art are also sprinkled all over our lives. When life offers a particularly captivating twist, we say, "It's like fiction." This expression is a manifestation of our deep-seated dream of a divine miracle and an admission of a disappointing disparity between the banal routine and the beautiful art.

Even today, despite its growing pragmatism the Russian world is not as *disenchanted* as its Western counterpart—that is, unlike in the West "the elimination of magic from the world's occurrences"[4] is still not embraced here. And while "Puritanism fundamentally turned away from all culture that appeals to the senses," as "all magical means to the quest for salvation [were ultimately understood] as superstition and sacrilege,"[5] in Russia miracles and mystery continue to imbue daily life. (How else to explain that Russians still wait for a "just czar" to come and fix their lives for them?)

For example, Nabokov's native Saint Petersburg, which was willfully brought into existence as an assurance of Russia's Westernism, is not even an exception that proves the rule—it just proves them: enchanting Petersburg is yet another ghost, the beautiful Russian fantasy of the West, not the West itself. If you take a guided tour of its canals, not only will your guide point out the apartments of Blok and Pushkin, he will show you where Raskolnikov[6] and Akaky Akakievich subsisted in great poverty, and along which streets Yevgeny fled the Bronze Horseman . . .

In Moscow, you'll spend hours searching for the house where Bulgakov's Margarita lived, as if she really lived there. In the Russian "high-context" culture image and narrative are not simply letters and words on the printed page but part of our life, our everyday, ordinary existence. In the Petersburg rain or the Moscow traffic, the stories of these lives, always full, always vital, complete our own, which we consider not nearly as interesting or dramatic. Russia's literary heroes, the writers who created them, and the readers who follow their destinies, invariably tend to become parameters of one single space—geographical, spiritual, and physical.

Thus, for nearly two centuries we've *lived* in Gogol and Dostoevsky, not distinguishing between fantasy and reality: we consciously swap fantasy for reality to avoid contact with the material and ordinary, to continue to live beyond physical bounds in our intensely spiritual world of the Orthodox religion, or the "earthly paradise" of communism. We stubbornly fenced off this world with borders, "no exit" signs, and slogans warning the collapse of our soulful culture, or our socialist purity, which we've opposed to Western rationalism and American imperialism.

Let me clarify for those who may think that "not distinguishing between fantasy and reality" doesn't apply to Vladimir Lenin's Bolshevik ideology because he and the other Marxists argued for the rational approach to Russian spiritual matters. Bolshevik rationalism had a distinctly utopian nature, which, in the words of Isaiah Berlin, resulted in "the mixture of utopian faith and brutal disregard for civilized morality."[7] In fact, the problem of Leninist communism was not that it was based upon Western rationalism or atheism (after all, the twentieth century has known many reasonably successful democratic socialist systems such as those of the Scandinavian countries and Holland), but that it too quickly succumbed to the Russian traditions of mysticism and obscurantism. Behind Stalin's collectivization of agriculture and the Soviet industrial exploits lay not Marxism but the social and moral-psychological tradition of the peasant communality of the *mir*.

But finally, sixteen years ago, when we became ready to exchange our communist collectivism for democratic individualism, it was time to turn to new authors and new role models, renouncing the typical Russian worldview of communal values, mysticism, and the suffering of the human soul, best defined by Fyodor Dostoevsky in his novels such as *The Idiot, The Devils,* and *The Brothers Karamazov.* These qualities, he promised, would guarantee Russia's moral victory over the rest of the world.

For those tired of waiting for the nineteenth-century writer's unfulfilled prophesies, twentieth-century Nabokov never looked better: Russian and Western, an aristocrat and an orphan (an exile), traditional (in the sense that he was heir to the Russian literary and cultural traditions) and modern, national (Russian, American, European—something for everyone), and international.

Rejecting Dostoevsky—"no, I do not object to soul-searching and self-revelation, but in those books [*The Brothers Karamazov* and *Crime and Punishment*] the soul, and the sins, and the sentimentality, and the journalese, hardly warrant the tedious and muddled search" (*SO,* I#13, 148)—Nabokov offered a more constructive, more aesthetic, and more practical variant of the search for self-conception. Nabokov showed others how to live now—in a world with open borders, among different people, different countries, and different cultures. He showed us how to live in the new solitude of multiple worlds.

But Nabokov's literary example would have remained incomplete, unrecognized, isolated, and irrelevant to Russia's painfully emerging capitalist consciousness without readers, without those of us who dared not only to read Nabokov, but to live him, to become his characters, and, finally, to attest that a writer can indeed converse with the future—it's only a matter of time before the right interlocutor turns up.

It turned out to be me. Instead of reaching my chosen writer through the "subjective limits" (*SM*, 69) he placed throughout his books, guarding his personal self with prefaces, forewords, conclusions, and afterwords, I took another tack, gaining entry to Nabokov's world via my own: "While trying to convey my attitude towards his art I have not produced any tangible proofs of its peculiar existence. I can only place my hand on my heart and affirm that I have not imagined [him]. He really wrote, he really lived" (*LORL*, 61).[8]

DEATH IS BUT A QUESTION OF STYLE

He who finds a new ending for a drama, with no death or exit,
will be the greatest man of all.
—Victor Shklovsky, *Energiya zabluzhdeniya*

Why had he moved to Switzerland?

Nabokov explained it this way: "There are . . . family reasons for our living in this part of Europe. I have a sister in Geneva and a son in Milan" (*SO*, I#4, 49).

But still, why had he settled in Montreux, a small town on the shores of Lake Geneva? The question gave me no peace from the moment I arrived. The country was marvelous, of course—lakes, mountains, cows, cheese, chocolate, watches, jewelry stores, churches, money, and banks. Everything is clean and orderly, the shrubbery and trees are pruned even in the woods, as if they were in model parks. And everything is illuminated by an incredible peacefulness, not even peacefulness so much as infinity, timelessness, eternity. For immortality it's marvelous, of course, but rather boring for living.

Nabokov was a famous writer, world-renowned, the author of the celebrated *Lolita* and *Speak, Memory,* a professor at Cornell University, a contributor to the *New Yorker,* the darling of journalists and a friend of Edmund Wilson, and now, after twenty successful years in America, not to mention earlier years (albeit maybe less successful) in such respected metropolises as Saint Petersburg, Berlin, and Paris, he moved into a hotel suite in a small resort town in a very small country.

"Why did he move here?" I asked myself as I entered Montreux one sunny September morning the year of Nabokov's centennial.

Critics, taking his lead, explain the move biographically: "Relatives in Europe. Montreux resembles the Mediterranean resorts where the Nabokovs spent summer months. Mountains and water are next to each other on a small piece of land. West European butterflies, different from Russian and East Coast U.S. species.

The country's central location was also important: Italy, France, and the Frankfurt Book Fair are all nearby—everyone would visit."[9]

As I drove down Grand-Rue, the town's main promenade, I had to accept the biographers' version: it was true—the beauty, the central location, the European atmosphere. And the luxury, of course—Nabokov would always remain a Russian aristocrat.

Which hotel was his? There was no lack of fashionable hotels in Montreux. All along Grand-Rue, one side facing the lake, the other rising into the mountains, hotels vied in luxury, grandeur, and size. I was looking for something small and exquisitely re-fined, suitable for the writer who hated large groups. After all, if you're going to live twenty years in a hotel, especially in a resort town, it would probably be in some pension, modest, homey, and far from the madding crowd.

Which then was Nabokov's? Before my eyes there arose a hulk of a hotel, which even by luxurious European standards was too luxurious: huge, much larger than anything around it, with or-nate balconies, filigree, and plaster carvings from the Silver Age of the last century. The architecture of Prague, Vienna, and Saint Pe-tersburg seemed like models of modernist modesty in comparison with the bright yellow cornices, eclectically scattered along the majestic façade of the Palace. The edifice resembled a very rich, expensive cake, with butter cream icing, which despite its glori-ousness was a bit too rich. The grandiose pomposity took my breath away.

Nevertheless, those sunny cornices had the amazingly attractive eccentricity and self-confidence typical of wealth, genius, and aristocracy. I recalled some lines from *Speak, Memory:* "From the age of seven, everything I felt in connexion with a rectangle of framed sunlight was dominated by a single passion. If my first glance of the morning was for the sun, my first thought was for the butterflies it would engender" (*SM*, 90), and had the fleeting thought, "Nabokov must have liked this place," as I vainly sought any signs of Nabokov's presence. After all, the famous writer had lived in Montreux for so many years. But for naught. It's amazing how calmly, not to say indifferently, the Swiss treat their celebrities, all the more foreign ones. Of course they know about Nabokov, they know that he spent almost twenty years in Switzerland, but it doesn't seem to elicit any particular delight. Big deal, Nabokov, so what?

They say that Charlie Chaplin, who lived in neighboring Vevey, moved to this country precisely because no one cared about his presence here, while England and France welcomed him with ovations, flowers, love, and adoration. It's not that the Swiss didn't know who Charlie Chaplin was—they are a cultured and educated people. But still, "Charlie Chaplin, so what?"

Undoubtedly, I myself should have known of the famous Montreux Palace, but Nabokov, who was in my mind larger than life, didn't seem to require such minutiae as his hotel information—it seemed too mundane. I somehow thought that at least the whole town, if not the whole country, especially for his hundredth birthday, would be his big (small, due to their size) literary museum.

The only way to find out where Nabokov lived was to go into one of the town's hotels in the hopes that the people there—polite and helpful—would have the necessary information for a less indifferent foreigner.

I decided on the glistening yellow cake. They'd be sure to have tourist brochures.

I bounded out of the car, entered the enormous and luxurious lobby, looked around and took a few steps, only to freeze. Before me, in a bronze chair, sat Nabokov.

Not at all how I had pictured him—the suave Russian aristocrat, the elegant British gentleman (a look picked up in Cambridge), the confident American professor, the exquisite European snob. He was almost sprawled in the chair, wearing a baggy jacket, vest and knickerbockers, aloofly staring off to one side. I had the feeling that sitting there, he was waiting for none other than me.

Like Martin in *Glory*, I was beckoned by the sunny hotel, and I came in response to that call: "What was it about that hotel that lured him so strongly? . . . But there was no doubt that it beckoned to him: the reflected sunlight in its windows flashed a silent sign of invitation. Martin was even frightened by such enigmatic intrusion, such abstruse insistence. . . . There he must go down: it would be wrong to ignore such blandishments" (*Glory*, 75).

Arriving without an invitation, even without a warning, but completely by accident and unerringly choosing the right place,

I deserved Nabokov's approval, even his trust, for proving the truth of his own theory that "intuition is a sesame of love" (*BS*, 207).

Of course, thirty years earlier he would not have forgiven such liberties—there were plenty who wanted to drop in without invitation and it wasn't the business of the hotel to select visitors—but now, plunged into eternal bronze meditation, he treated my impertinence with surprising geniality.

Speak, Memory opens with a description of a young man who finds the black abyss of prenatal existence more frightening than the black abyss of postmortal nonexistence. An empty baby carriage in a homemade movie scares him to death: dead, he is certain to leave behind a great writer, but never being born, he can't become Nabokov.

With his bronze tranquility, Vladimir Vladimirovich confirmed this obvious but rarely expressed truth—before birth a person doesn't know his place in the world and that frightens him. After death, his position is defined, which frees him forever of anxiety and restlessness. Nabokov will now for ever and ever sit in the bronze chair in the Palace Hotel, in Montreux, Switzerland.

"Why did you move here?" I asked after some hesitation in English. There was nothing Slavic in that detached and inaccessible figure, who had consciously switched from the language of stormy Russian passions to inscrutable English. I knew that he spoke Russian only to his intimates. My brand of Russian, on the other hand, to his taste was probably too polluted by Sovietspeak.

"You see," he replied unexpectedly in our native tongue. (Thousands of people had come to worship him, a twentieth-century classic. While I had come to visit, simply to visit Vladimir Nabokov, a writer, and he who had written *Glory* must have appreciated my boldness. "Unless of course," an unwelcome thought zipped through my mind, "he is so completely bored to death in this monumental eternity that he welcomes even the slightest distraction.")

"You must have noticed by now that nothing ever happens in Switzerland. It is neutral in all respects. **No bothersome demonstrations, no spiteful strikes. Alpine butterflies. Fabulous sunsets—just west of my window, spangling the lake, splitting the crimson sun! Also, the pleasant surprise of a metaphorical sunset in charming surroundings.**[10] And now my monument has forever become part of this magnificently beautiful monotony," he smiled.

"Russia, you know, can at any moment turn back, rush off to the left, the right, rear up, and, as is its habit, erase any slices of time that are inconvenient for new ideologies, as it did long ago in 1917 or more recently in 1991. America . . . America is developing with such speed that in the final analysis, without wanting to, it must constantly *recycle* (that is what you call that now?) old memories, old idols, in order to free up space for the continuously appearing new ones, who instantly vanish in their turn. I'm not even speaking of the constant weather cataclysms—floods, earthquakes, and fires—that replace there the catastrophes of revolution.

"But perhaps you'd like some tea?" he said with sudden hospitality.

"We usually have tea in the music room. Without music, of course. I'm not a great music lover, you know. I prefer chess." Nabokov regarded me dubiously. He must have thought that since I didn't know his hotel, then I might not know about chess, or musical allusions, or perhaps, even the butterflies. I was embarrassed, but it would have been stupid to explain that I had read, knew, and understood. How else could I have guessed which was his hotel? And now, hearing a train pulling away from the station on the neighboring Rue de la Gare, I knew for sure why he had moved here—stations and "trains with fabulous destination" (*Glory*, 133), those "infinitely long-distance trains" (*G*, 170) had always captivated him, as they captivated Martin Edelweiss and Fyodor Godunov-Cherdyntsev, those cosmopolitan doubles of little Volodya, young Sirin, and today's eminent Vladimir Nabokov.

Not seeming to notice my confusion, Nabokov continued, "We moved into a lovely small section of the hotel, originally a separate building, which was still called by its original name, the Cygne, and the Palace itself always seemed just a luxurious neighbor to us. **We dwell in the older part of the Palace Hotel, in its original part really, which was all that existed a hundred and fifty years ago (you can still see that initial inn and our future windows in old prints of 1840 or so)."**[11]

"But let's get back to chess. It is as creative as music, but it's quieter, calmer, wiser. Its problems **demand from the composer the same virtues that characterize all worthwhile art: originality, invention, harmony, conciseness, complexity, and splendid insincerity.**[12] You have read *Zashchita Luzhina*, of course?" he asked. Blushing, I nodded: of course! "Our music room is very beautiful. Once its walls were painted with Russian landscapes. I feel almost at home here."

At home? Nabokov always said that his unwillingness to have a house (he didn't acquire real estate even in more than ten years at Cornell) stemmed from the fact that once you've had one, all the rest can be only pathetic imitations, a vain attempt to fill uniquely beautiful memories with banal content. The hotel, juxtaposed with one's "own" house, was in all his books the symbol of unanchored homelessness and the illusory nature of existence. It is a forced heaven and a sign of bitter freedom, in which man, having lost paradise forever, is merely a guest on earth with no reason to accumulate heavy life baggage. Like trains and stations, hotels free one from belonging to a specific place on earth, in exchange connecting all the places of the Nabokovian spectral universe.

In *Glory*, Martin "noted a certain peculiarity about his life: the property that his reveries had of crystallizing and mutating into reality, as previously they had mutated into sleep" (*Glory*, 108–9). And for Vladimir Nabokov the writer, the hotels that were considered, described, symbolized, dreamed over, and lived in *The Defense, Glory,* and *King, Queen, Knave* became incarnate in the novel of his own life as the six-story sunny and wonderful Montreux Palace, replacing Russian cozy warmth with Swiss static constancy.

"A very old Russian friend of ours, now dwelling in Paris, remarked recently when she was here, that one night, forty years ago, in the course of a little quiz at one of her literary parties in Berlin, I, being asked where I would like to live, answered, 'In a large comfortable hotel.'[13] A real gem in my collection of premonitions and future retrospectives,[14] don't you think?" he smiled with confidence.

"You see," Nabokov continued . . .

I had already grown accustomed to that slow introduction, condescending and simultaneously leading you into the rhythm of his thought, speech, immortality. "Switzerland is the closest place to the heavens on earth. It is an earthly paradise in miniature—urban civilization, a civilized village, eternal snows, Mediterranean climate—and such an ideal combination on a small slice of territory is possible only here. Look at those mountains, that lake, the trees and flowers; at this idyllic tranquility, this beauty of eternity. Switzerland is almost unreal, because it never changes; it is neutral, constant, and infinite.

"Existing in space, at a specific latitude and longitude, with roads, cities, and railroad stations, being at the intersection of all roads, verticals and horizontals (the rue de la Gare is always the central street here), it is simultaneously outside events. This minimal spaciousness reveals a broad expanse of time, especially in a resort city, where space becomes an exclusively temporal phenomenon, not part of life but a vacation from it.

"Switzerland is remarkable because here you are enveloped in a heavenly sense of freedom, on the condition, of course, that you remain a tourist. I am a tourist, a hotel guest, and to the highest degree this creates my anonymity, alienation, and aloofness. I am here and not here simultaneously, which **confirms me in my favorite habit—the habit of freedom.**[15]

"In compressing space to the minimum, time expands infinitely," he concluded significantly.

"Is that why the Swiss are so fixated on time?" I said with a nod.

"No, not on time, on clocks, the skeleton of time," Nabokov corrected me. "You see, as I've already noted, nothing ever happens here. In other places governments fall, war, earthquake, and avalanche roar, flood and fire rumble, revolutions shock and volcanoes erupt, always presenting a not necessarily pleasant but always accurate starting point for calculating time and ages. The Swiss must depend on the accuracy of their **chronometrical**[16] mechanisms to find themselves within time. How else can they distinguish the sixteenth century from the twenty-sixth? They have to count on the most elaborate clock face designs, following the process of human time, reflecting the latest fashions and technological innovations."

Nabokov smiled gently, as if to apologize for his sarcasm about the Swiss, who did not even suspect, poor things, that "applied time—time applied to events, which we measure by means of clocks and calendars" (*SO*, I#19, 185)—in fact had nothing to do with the "true reality" (ibid., I#9, 118). He never apologized to his readers for his scorn, did not apologize to other writers for his arrogance (with the exception of a few greats—Pushkin, Gogol), in other words, he did not apologize. But he apologized to the Swiss, probably because from his vantage point of genius and eternity contemplating everything temporal and material, he was generous to those who indeed were capable of creating an earthly paradise—boring, may be, but how much more livable than that destructive paradise of the Gulag dreamed up by Lenin-Trotsky-Stalin.

"So, here I am absolutely free to concentrate on the temporal category, the most important in my opinion for life, and death, and history," Nabokov continued. "**I confess I do not believe in time. I like to fold my magic carpet . . . in such a way as to superimpose one part of the pattern upon another. . . . And the highest enjoyment of timelessness—in a landscape selected at random—is when I stand among rare butterflies and their food plants.**[17]

"All my heroes, especially those born in Switzerland, are always from mysterious, unreal places 'selected at random'—Kinbote in *Pale Fire* is from strange Zembla, Ada and Van Veen in *Ada* come from Ladoga, Kaluga, Kitezh, Raduga, such Russian place names transported to the Western Hemisphere.

"Place, you know, is a conditional category, it exists only as much as time, memory, and eternity exist. **In some peculiar way**

Space is merely the waste product of Time.[18] Thanks to time, Adam Krug [in *Bend Sinister*] returns to the city of his childhood, philosophical discoveries, dead wife, the city that exists geographically but has ceased to exist, renamed by the tyrannical Paduk as totalitarian Padukgrad."

Nabokov fell silent, meditating heavily on the fate of Krug, probably the most horrible of all that befell his heroes. By cruel chance losing his son, the only remaining bridge between Krug's former country and Paduk's present-day, Adam is forced to watch the videotape of the child's murder. But then his pitying creator liberates his hero from "the senseless agony of his logical fate" (*BS*, 233), and generously returns him to the author's consciousness, to the "comparative paradise" of the writer's study with "the bedside lamp, the sleeping tablets, the glass of milk" (*BS*, 241).

Awakening from his deep meditation, Nabokov went on, "Place is conditional, it can always be changed—from Russia to Padukgrad, through America and Switzerland to my desk. . . . But time can't be changed, it can't be finished, it can only be developed, through the rebirth of the past in a new time, and so on to infinity, adding new turns to the endless spiral.

"In *Ada*, Van Veen did a thorough study of the relationship between time and space and concluded: '**One can be a hater of Space, and a lover of Time**.'[19] In a world of vanishing countries and cultures, murdered children and destroyed adults, only time can overcome losses, separation, and their result, death. Time, real time, always exists in the perspective of history and infinity simultaneously. **Time, though akin to rhythm, is not simply rhythm, which would imply motion—and Time doesn't move. Van's greatest discovery is his perception of Time as the dim hollow between two rhythmic beats, the narrow and bottomless silence *between* the beats, not the beats themselves, which only embar Time. In this sense human life is not a pulsating heart but the missed heartbeat.**[20] I hope you understand what I am saying?" he asked, with the same gentle condescension.

I understood. I understood that this was why in every Nabokov novel without exception clocks, their faces, their tones, their visibility in physical space are noted by the author, the characters, and the readers—in marking the passage of time, they, these chronometrical mechanisms, create the illusion of immediate reality without which even the most oblique and tangential contact with what we call life is impossible. But counting time "mercilessly," "senselessly," and "trivially" (descriptions of clocks in *Invitation to a Beheading*), they only confuse the essence of real time—eternity, immortality, death—by limiting it to a spatial category.

"Krug . . . wandering through the rooms of the deserted cottage whose two clocks . . . are probably still going, alone, intact, pathetically sticking to man's notion of time after man has gone" (*BS*, 111), continues the thoughts of Cincinnatus C., written two novels earlier: "not only am I still alive, that is, the sphere of my own self still limits and eclipses my being" (*ITB*, 89), while Cincinnatus in turn agrees with Luzhin, who even earlier "accepted this external life as something inevitable but completely uninteresting" (*LD*, 95).

"**We, poor Spatians, are better adapted . . . to Extension rather than to Duration,**"[21] Nabokov said musingly, setting down his empty cup. "Places, clocks, bodies—these are all categories of materialization. They are a constant source of physical imperfection, of numerical and objective count that separates us from the reality of eternity. I have always suspected that **the impersonal darkness on both sides of my life . . . is caused merely by the walls of time separating me . . . from the free world of timelessness.**[22] And now, as I sit in this bronze chair, I am completely confident that I was right.

"The ability to fold the magic carpet in any stretch of time is the only way to gain access to immortality. When my little son picked up on a beach **small bits of pottery, still beautiful in glaze and color . . .** I did **not doubt that among those slightly convex chips of majolica ware found by our child there was one whose border of scroll-work fitted exactly, and continued, the pattern of a fragment I had found in 1903 on the same shore, and that the two tallied with a third my mother had found on that Mentone beach in 1882, and with a fourth piece of the same pottery that had been found by *her* mother a hundred years ago—and so on, until this assortment of parts, if all had been preserved, might have been put together to make the complete, the absolutely complete, bowl, broken by some Italian child God** knows where and when, and now mended by *these* rivets of bronze."[23]

I dared to interrupt, "The bronze bowl was left in the past, and by these shores, in a new coil of the spiral, its fragments formed a bronze statue."

Nabokov nodded in approval. **"The spiral is a spiritualized circle. In the spiral form, the circle, uncoiled, unwound, has ceased to be vicious; it has been set free.**[24] We've all come out of Gogol's 'Overcoat,'" he said with a smile.

I smiled back, knowing his disparaging attitude toward Dostoevsky but not really knowing how to react to this abrupt switch in the conversation. Apparently, Nabokov had no intention of discussing his literary prejudices, but instead was revealing, with his usual condescension but also with astonishing concern, the background of his characters.

"You see, we've all come out of Russian culture, and my characters have come out of Russian literature, out of *Anna Karenina, The Idiot, The Diary of a Madman*. . . . We all found ourselves in another age, at another longitude and latitude, tossed onto other shores on the next postrevolutionary coil of the spiral. But the language was our handicap. It was getting in the way of a new transforming hero, preventing this hero from understanding the virtues of a straight and simple line, word, rule, sentence. It metastasized with endless lyrical digressions, fenced and circled itself with parentheses and commas, sprouted semicolons and dashes all over the never-ending volumes, covering all our eleven time zones. Snowdrifts of suffering and excitement prevented the determined and driven individual who was free from all emotional reflections from moving on. The useless and impractical knowledge of a Russian intellectual required retooling into better practical skills in **efficient, alabastrine, humane America.**[25]

"Remember Pnin?" continued Nabokov in English: "**He was inept with his hands to a rare degree; but because he could manufacture in a twinkle a one-note mouth organ out of a pea pod, make a flat pebble skip ten times on the surface of a pond, shadowgraph with his knuckles a rabbit (complete with blinking eye), and perform a number of other tame tricks that Russians have up their sleeves, he believed himself endowed with considerable manual and mechanical skill.**"[26]

Just like his Pnin, exiled from the kindness of the communal paradise of Russian literature, Nabokov too had to adjust, conform to other shores, to another language, to the comfortably individualistic Western adult "hell" that replaced his cozy native Russian paradise.

Impassive Nabokov paused to reflect again. "Martin, who had learned early to control his tears and conceal his emotions, astonished his schoolteachers with his insensibility," I recalled a passage from *Glory* (13). The Russian author most unsympathetic to and scornful of human frailty wore an unabashed mask of indifference—"In America I'm happier than in any other country" (*SO,* I#2, 10).

And still . . . he suffered unbearably from the loss of his native tongue, his native home, his native land:

> *But now thou too must go; just here we part,*
> *Softest of tongues, my true one, all my own . . .*
> *And I am left to grope for heart and art*
> *And start anew with clumsy tools of stone.*[27]

Even the word *rodno*i in Russian has overtones of family and closeness that are almost completely lost in English translation as *native, familial, own.* Like Adam Krug, Nabokov could return to the country of his childhood in time and memory but not in space, forced to replace movement with thought: "One is always at home in one's past" (*SM*, 87).

In *Speak, Memory,* Nabokov muses: "I wonder, by the way, what would happen if I put in a long distance call [to 24-43, the old phone number of the Nabokovs in Saint Petersburg] from my desk right now? No answer? No such number? No such country?" (*SM*, 182–83).

In the Russian version, *Drugie berega,* he confesses: "Longing for home. It has its clutches, that longing, in a small corner of the world, and it can be pulled away only by killing it. . . . Give me, on any continent, a forest, meadow, and air that resemble the province of Saint Petersburg, and my soul gets turned inside out" (*DB*, 270–71).

"He didn't love . . . his country because he had lost it. But he loved [it] most deeply in [its] loss, and his love is most alive in the imagining . . . of the Russia he will never see again. He loved the chance of loss, he loved what he *could* lose, which is perhaps what we really love in anyone or anything,"[28] Michael Wood, a literary scholar from Princeton University, explains in his book on Nabokov. And "that loss is irredeemable, that loss goes on and on."[29]

As pain, as life, as death. . . .

If Nabokov had not been Russian but a purely Western individual, he would not have perceived life on the other shore as a cruel necessity. Then it would have been an indisputable given, with no longing for the paradisiacal past, his homeland, his home. But it is precisely that unforgettable, unhealing wound of loss, the source of constant pain that determined the immortality of the writer and his books.

What can be said of a paradise that is not lost, for it becomes paradise only once it is no longer there? Deprived of Russia, Nabokov loved it even more and learned to overcome the pain in endless reminiscences of Zembla, Kaluga, Ladoga that moved from novel to novel, confirming Michael Wood's "lost love" theory: "it is all a matter of love: the more you love a memory, the stronger and stranger it is. I think it's natural that I have a more passionate affection for my old memories, the memories of my childhood" (*SO*, I#2, 12).

According to Nabokov, loss—this death of hopes and dreams—could be overcome by an aptly directed, precisely calculated spiral repetition of already familiar themes, images, situations, only bettered, improved, straightened, "happyfied": "pattern is a redemption of loss, and perhaps the only redemption of loss there is."[30]

The exploit of death—the Russian end—became Nabokov's exploit of life—the Western wellspring. Rewriting Gogol, Dostoevsky, and Tolstoy in accordance with his own sobering experience of Westernization, he escapes the vicious circle of misery sketched by Russian cultural tradition.

Nabokov took on the most difficult task of all his riddles—logically, constructively, like a chess problem or a complicated puzzle, to solve the riddle of the circled composition of Russian unhappiness, mistaken for spiritual uniqueness. He ventured to find a defense from the constantly repeating thematic pattern of Russian literature and Russian life, the basis of which is patient pain, thunderous revolution, heroic death. Nabokov had to remake, to fix this clock mechanism, broken many times over, this wrecked time machine with worn out bits and batteries—this Russian theme of life for the sake of death, in which measured happiness was not even a desirable constant.

"The spiral is a spiritualized circle," he seemed to completely forget about my presence, "In the spiral form, the circle, uncoiled, unwound, has ceased to be vicious; it has been set free."

Banishing his Russian heroes from their all-forgiving culture, not merely tolerant of pain but brought up on it, growing and flourishing in suffering, taking away the comfort of the release brought by a heroic escape, Nabokov makes them begin a new life much more horrible than the one from which compassionate

Russian literature had so generously protected them: merciless Western life after merciful Russian death. Just as Nabokov himself once was, on the new, contemporary coil of the spiral, they are forced to adjust to the new, much more difficult conditions of open space, freedom of choice, responsibility for one's fate, and the necessity of making one's own decisions. He deprives them of the comfort of their native tongue, the Russian coziness of parentheses, colons, dashes, and commas behind which one can hide as if behind a gate, hunker down behind a fence, buffered from life's wind, blanketed by fluffy snow as if it were an eiderdown—we'll wait it out, winter over, survive till better times . . .

"And a sentence begun somewhere once upon a time in another time and space spins and turns and twists around itself in the typical ring architecture of a Russian village, in the ring composition of *Dead Souls*,[31] and you can't see the beginning from the end, and only the familiar bell finishes its jingle, and here we are in a different dimension, far away and still in the same place. Striving to get from the wheel to the flying troika, from war to peace, from Pushkin to Onegin, we describe an arc and come back to the beginning, to the wheel and to Pushkin.[32]

"And then, bored by the measured process of evolution, we rush to tear the ring with thunderous revolution, sweeping everything in its path. And then, resting from the shocks, we wait again for centuries for spring to come and the blizzard to pass outside the window, beyond the line, in the other, rectilinear world.

"There a naked man on bare soil would not rhyme *dolya* (fate, lot) with *volya* (freedom, will)[33] as if they were synonyms, does not play up to Nature and, covered head to toe, hope for pity from Her. He marches into the wind, takes decisions and executes them, despite the bad weather and the poor harvest. . . .[34] Western man, *homo economicus* and English-speaking, rectilinear, who has no place to hide in this bare and rational land, has no choice but to conquer the land rationally and egotistically. He takes his Western fate in his masterful, willful hands and proves that '**All happy families are more or less dissimilar; all unhappy ones are more or less alike.**'[35] (The only thing you Russians know how to do is suffer!)

"The Western individual is practical, he doesn't seek relief in madness, revolution, death, suicide, or escape into the void. He does not elevate pain and suffering into the meaning and basis of existence. For him death is not a way out, not a grand exploit of relief—he lives from day to day, from yesterday to today, from today to tomorrow, and so on to the end, slowly, forced to experience the ordinariness and triteness of life as the evolutionary given of the human condition."

Followers of Nabokov and heirs of Poprishchin (Kinbote in *Pale Fire*), Karenina and Levin (Ada and Van Veen in *Ada, or Ardor*), Prince Myshkin (Cincinnatus C. in *Invitation to a Beheading*), and Ivanov (Timofey Pnin in *Pnin*), they enter into misery and misfortune as if these were not merely a result of hardships but the given of their existence.[36] Their life begins in that interface of death-eternity where the heroes of classical Russian literature ended theirs, at the moment when Poprishchin and Myshkin finally got rid of life. For Nabokov death is not only an end, it is the start of pain.

The forever-young Lolita once observed with all seriousness, "You know, what's so dreadful about dying is that you are completely on your own" (*Lolita*, 284), but truth be told, in Western living you are equally on your own. . . . On that same painful coil the happiness of Ada and Van Veen is no less horrible than Anna Karenina's tragic end—the novel's title speaks for itself (*ad* is Russian for hell). Their happiness is even more horrible, it is unhappiness, madness: trapped in the branches of a complex genealogical tree, the relationship of the willful cousins was clear only to themselves—incestuous love, cruel in its absolute nature, terrible in its urgent determination to be happy at any cost. Because it is "*in other more deeply moral worlds than this pellet of muck, there might exist restraints, principles, transcendental consolations, and even a certain pride in making happy someone one does not really love; but on* this *planet Lucettes are doomed*" (*Ada*, 498).

Hostages to their individual passions, Ada and Van can keep a happy balance only in their tight world of incest, circled completely around each other, and for that they are compelled to tease their younger sister, Lucette, to death. And the difference between the Veens, *polozhitelnye* (positive) characters, and Humbert (*Lolita*), an *otritsatelnyi* (negative) character, was just that their incest was an act of free will for both, while underage and inexperienced Lolita was manipulated into a romance with her stepfather.

In our age of "the mug of modernism" (*G*, 149) this obvious hell can be called a paradise. In this age, in fact, one can be even proud of the ability to adjust to that hell, because in the cold world of banal rationality happiness is what a person invents for himself; how happy he decides to assess his life.

"I will let you in on a little secret," Nabokov whispered, leaning closer, "You see, Humbert Humbert is horrible, because he himself believes he is horrible, while the witty Clare Quilty, an impotent lover of lovely girls, instead inspires those girls' unwavering admiration. Remember the pedophilic Gaston Godin: **his existence had such a queer bearing on** Humbert's case. **There he was, devoid of any talent whatsoever, a mediocre teacher, a worthless scholar, a glum repulsive fat old invert, highly contemptuous of the American way of life, triumphantly ignorant of the English language—there he was in priggish New England, crooned over by the old and caressed by the young—oh, having a grand time and fooling everybody; and here was**[37] Humbert. . . ."

We were the only ones left in the music room. The conversation, like the sunny day, was drawing to a close. It was time to say good-bye, thank him, and leave. . . .

"For a Russian hero," Nabokov said, stopping me, "death is not simply a salvation, but the justification for his petty, miserable, suffering life. After all, pain for us"—he paused and corrected himself—"for you," and after another pause, "for them, is a reward and suffering is a holiday. Look at how they die, leave, lose their minds, with the pathos of a tragic character—'I'll die, and then they'll. . . . They didn't understand me, they didn't appreciate me'—Bashmachkin, the Karamazovs, Ivan Ilyich."

Feeling sympathy for the heroes of the Russian classics, he did not forgive them their weakness and nonresistance: "Do you think you know the horror of suffering, real pain? I'll show you real pain, when even death holds no promise of an end to it!"

"But how I don't want to die! My soul has burrowed under the pillow. Oh, I don't want to! It will be cold getting out of my warm body. I don't want to . . . wait a while . . . let me doze some more" (*ITB*, 26), cries out Cincinnatus C. But having overcome the cold uncertainty of immortality, he bravely makes "his way in that direction where, to judge by the voices, stood beings akin to him" (ibid., 223).

Adam Krug after all his trials "comfortably returns unto the bosom of his maker" (*BS*, xix).

Pnin, perhaps the character Nabokov respected the most, who dared to be kinder and braver than the author (so unusual a feature that the entire novel about him was included in the anthology *The Portable Nabokov*), does not give in to humiliation and proudly rides off into nothingness.

Luzhin does not go mad from chess, as the critics have it: born into the madness of life with its insoluble problems at every step, "realizing that he had got stuck, that he had lost his way in one of the combinations he had so recently pondered, [he] made a desperate attempt to free himself, to break out somewhere" (*LD*,

140). He thus finds the only brilliant defense against life's madness—nonexistence.

And Nabokov, who spent his life rewriting the heroes of Russian literature in the hope of making his own "favorite creatures, [his] resplendent characters—in *The Gift*, in *Invitation to a Beheading*, in *Ada*, in *Glory*, et cetera . . . victors in the long run" (*SO*, I#19, 193), to reward them with a good ending for their courage to live, himself settled in the illusory paradise of Switzerland to finally compose the paradisiacal *Ada* with its absolute formula for individual happiness: "All happy families are more or less dissimilar."

> . . . if there were no future, then one had the right of
> making up a future, and in that case one's very own future
> did exist, insofar as one existed oneself. (*Ada*, 585)

Nabokov went on slowly: "And you will have to accept that pain is not an exploit, not a constant celebration, not a relapse, but an ordinary condition, the trivial norm of human existence. Death may be a way out, but without fanfare, thunder, sensationalism, and martyr's crown, it is not a happy escape but an almost inconspicuous, quiet disappearance, disintegration, a release not forever but for a time from the cruel horror of life until its next beginning, the new, evolutionary coil of the spiral.

"Death is either the instantaneous gaining of perfect knowledge . . . or absolute nothingness, *nichto*. . . . [38] And what on earth does it matter? . . . **Death is but a question of style**,"[39] Nabokov concluded in English.

He was lost in thought again. His death—"a mere literary device" (*BS*, xviii), one of the most exquisite in Russian literature—the Montreux Palace, a gem of modernism, his nonchalant bronze figure inside,[40] *Vladimir Nabokov écrivain* on his tombstone—was still not as seamless as Pushkin's end (the only classic author on whom Nabokov wrote commentary without rewriting), which was less stylized but more stylish, perfectly in tune with Pushkin's genius for elegance, humor and taste—a Frenchman, a beauty, a duel, a button, an anecdote—the sun of Russian poetry.[41]

The sun set, spangling the lake, and its last dying reflections glittered on the windows of the Palace, casting an evening glow that softened the yellow of the cornices. Politely letting me know that my audience was over, Nabokov bade me a brief farewell and invited me to drop in if I was ever in the neighborhood again.

I really wanted to ask him what our conversation had meant, why he had spoken to me about things he usually concealed carefully and hid on the smooth, brilliant surface of his novels, with "the mirror-like angles of his clear but weirdly misleading sentences" (*SM*, 225), why he had decided to speak to me in Russian, his intimate, sacred, native language, why . . .

But I was no longer there.

Nabokov sat alone, bronze, silent, indifferently gazing off to the side, into eternity, the great and arrogant Nabokov, author of *Lolita* and *Speak, Memory, Onegin* and *Gogol, Ada* and *Pale Fire*, Nabokov who translated, rewrote, added forewords, commentaries, and indexes to his novels, Nabokov who explained everything but revealed nothing, the scornful and brilliant classic of our time, totally immersed in his monumental exclusivity.

AFTERWORD (BUT NOT THE END)

Of all the characters that a great artist creates, his readers are the best.
—Vladimir Nabokov, *Lectures on Russian Literature*

In the tradition of Herman (*Despair*), V. (*The Real Life of Sebastian Knight*), Humbert Humbert (*Lolita*), Kinbote (*Pale Fire*), and all Nabokov's characters who are made to tell their own tale, I too, after narrating mine, was returned unto the bosom of my maker, to the beginning of my story to stand in front of the bronze statue, wondering whether this conversation had taken place at all. Or was it the reverberations of the Commendatore's footsteps[42] and the Bronze Horseman's hooves resounding traditionally on my Russian literary conscience where art and reality are indivisible?

But whether it did or did not happen is not for me to decide: an obedient protagonist of a commentary to eternity, which Nabokov made up to pass this very eternity, I had to follow the logic of his plot.

However, in order to make it easier on you, reader, I marked out some quotations, which originally appeared in his earlier published books. Nabokov, no doubt, would not have approved, as he once said, "the reader has to work in his turn. . . . Art is difficult" (*SO*, I#9, 115). He would have preferred you to ponder and try to recall where this or that phrase came from, but I, using my prerogative as a formal narrator, dared to disregard the will of my author.

I was unable to find everything we talked about in the body of his works, but this I am sure, was Nabokov's intention, a literary trick, consistent with his usual "introductions to" and "notes on," designed as brilliant chess problems in their endless mirror-like reflections: it seems that the answer is almost found, but it is not nearly enough to solve the original problem, so you are left to solve the reflection of the original, and then the reflection of the reflection, and so it continues, to infinity.

> The only thing he knew for sure was that from time immemorial he had been playing chess—and in the darkness of his memory, as in two mirrors reflecting a candle, there was only a vista of converging lights with Luzhin sitting at a chessboard, and again Luzhin at a chessboard, only smaller, and then smaller still, and so on an infinity of times. (*LD*, 135)

In the magician's wonderlands, his critics are as helpless as Alice on the corkscrew path to the garden: the closer we try to get to Nabokov, the further the answers recede. Always thinking the answer is at hand we come to see that our hopes for clarity will always be dashed:

> An observer makes a detailed picture of the whole universe but when he has finished he realizes that it still lacks

something: his own self. So he puts himself in it too. But again a 'self' remains outside and so forth, in an endless sequence of projections, like those advertisements which depict a girl holding a picture of herself holding a picture of herself holding a picture that only coarse printing prevents one's eye from making out. (OCE, 254)

Since our "I" is condemned to remain forever outside the bounds of Nabokov's universe, there is only one solution, I found, to his "mirror of being" (*BS*, xii) riddle—Vladimir Nabokov himself. The writer, who will never, either in prefaces, or in conclusions, or in forewords, or in commentaries, or even in conversations, explain to you anything that you are unable to understand yourself: "My inventions, my circles, my special islands are infinitely safe from exasperated readers" (*SO*, A#4, 241). And if by chance he chooses to reveal a few of his secrets, he will immediately add, "Nor have I ever yielded to the wild desire to thank a benevolent critic—or at least to express somehow my tender awareness of this or that friendly writer's sympathy and understanding, which in some extraordinary way seem always to coincide with talent and originality, an interesting, though not quite inexplicable phenomenon" (ibid.).

He then will promptly remind you that all phenomena are illusory anyway; that the boundary between reality and art is deceptive and indistinct. As it is indistinguishable between life and death, happiness and unhappiness, time and space, and so on and so forth—spirally, endlessly, eternally . . .

I think that what I would welcome at the close of a book of mine is a sensation of its world receding in the distance and stopping somewhere there, suspended afar like a picture in a picture: *The Artist's Studio* by Van Bock. (*SO*, I#6, 72–73)[43]

TWO

On the Way to the Author

*A good reader is bound to make fierce efforts when wrestling
with a difficult author.*
—Vladimir Nabokov, *Strong Opinions*

HOW IT BEGAN

I've read Nabokov before.

First, it was *Lolita* in his own Russian translation; forbidden
pages passed from hand to hand in pale green, cardboard-bound
facsimile. I was exactly the same age as the heroine. And I
hated her.

Later, during perestroika, there was *The Luzhin Defense*—
printed abroad in Ardis's "zagranichnoe" (attractive foreign)
edition—it made an impression, but I didn't finish it. I wasn't yet
ready, although I could already feel its force and genius.

In 1988, *The Gift* was published officially in the literary
journal *Ural*. I didn't finish it either: Chernyshevsky's[1] aesthetic
creed—ideological art is the highest art—and his ascetic hero

Rakhmetov had always been boring. But Nabokov's antihero—the self-assured and athletic Godunov-Cherdyntsev, who, scornful of everything and everyone, poked merciless fun at Chernyshevsky—wasn't any more entertaining. In the late 1980s, it was still not clear that an ethos of individual, anticommunal snobbery suited our not-yet-pragmatic age any better than extravagant Russian civic-mindedness; that the "rational egoism" of a modern *Hero of Our Time*[2] was more relevant than the didactic moralism of *What Is to Be Done?*

Then I started *Mary,* which was first published in Russia at about the same time as *The Gift.* Again, I didn't finish it: its purposeful heroes (after the type of *Oblomov*'s Shtoltz)[3] didn't interest me. They were far removed from our still Soviet reality, moribund as it may have been. This was the romantic Gorbachev era and, as before, we were striving to remake the world into a benevolent brotherhood—communism with a human face—for the sake of high ideals. So Ganin struck me as false and conceited, strongly resembling, as I suspected even then, his creator Vladimir Nabokov. We loved weak but kindhearted, "genuine" Russian heroes—Ilyusha Oblomov, Akaky Akakievich, Petya Trofimov . . . [4] Making an exception for Pushkin, we also preferred writers who were content to be "authors," whose "self-promoting" memoirs and opinions weren't necessarily commentaries on and addenda to most of their books.

Around 1995, I reread *Lolita,* this time in English and in America. It shook me to the depths of my soul. Another book unfinished, but this time from shock: How did he do it? How does one write like that in a foreign language? These perfect, shining, chiseled, masterfully etched American landscapes, thoughts, phrases, and words were themselves a wonder, all the more so for having been written by a foreigner—by a European, by a Russian. I was getting lost in its wandering and its language: "Now, in perusing what follows, the reader should bear in mind not only the general circuit as adumbrated above, with its many sidetrips and tourist traps, secondary circles and skittish deviations, but also the fact that far from being an indolent *partie de plaisir,* our tour was a hard, twisted, teleological growth" (*Lolita,* 154).

But most shocking of all was that for all its foreignness—linguistic and whatnot—at times *Lolita* felt like Russian literature. Nabokov's English hadn't completely nullified his Russian way of thinking. Behind the graceful Western constructions and the ornaments of provincial America, I could make out the ever vanishing, shifting contours of a Russian poet-seer who's remade the Western world, his former homeland casting long shadows upon his new.

"I didn't know any American twelve-year-old girls, and I did not know America; I had to invent America and Lolita" (*SO,* I#3, 26), explained Nabokov in one interview, insisting in another that "artistic originality has only its own self to copy" (ibid., I#7, 95).

In his postscript to *Lolita,* Nabokov lamented:

My private tragedy . . . is that I had to abandon my natural idiom, my untrammeled, rich, and infinitely docile

Russian tongue for a second-rate brand of English, devoid of any of those apparatuses—the baffling mirror, the black velvet backdrop, the implied associations and traditions—which the native illusionist, frac-tails flying, can magically use to transcend the heritage in his own way. (*Lolita*, 316–17)

Whatever doubts he may have had about his English, he was to "transcend the heritage in his own way"—and "magically" at that. Fretting that "in the hands of a harmful drudge, the Russian version of *Lolita* would be entirely degraded and botched by vulgar paraphrases and blunders" (*SO*, I#3, 38), he simply translated the novel himself, ensuring that none of the magic was wasted in his native language. Still, eight years later, in the "Postscript to the Russian Edition," Nabokov admitted:

The story of this translation is a story of disillusionment. Alas, that "remarkable Russian language," which I'd believed was waiting for me somewhere all this time—blooming like a sure springtime beyond tightly locked gates to which I'd kept the key so many years—doesn't really exist. Beyond the gates are nothing but charred stumps and the barren expanse of fall, and the key in my hand is more like a crowbar.[5]

Though I felt the writer's loss, I couldn't entirely accept his linguistic complaints. Given his ability to travel back and forth so freely between the images, words, and concepts of various languages, one couldn't help but wonder whether Nabokov's anguish over his vanished Russian was nothing more than a pose. The painstaking (where's our native "avos da nebos"? [hope for an off-chance probability]) translation of *Lolita*, and the novel's stylistic enchantment in either language, belied Nabokov's sham loss of fluency. These feelings, even if personally sincere, were also professionally (maybe too professionally, I thought) formulated for public consumption.

I say leave the rewording to the experts. Great artists should be generous—not cling to each of their words as if to the highest truth. Take for example Abram Tertz:

> You toss [an essay] aside (in the air, almost) and say casually "I've finished" and listen to criticism. . . . But by then you don't care. It lives. Once born, it lives independently of you, asking no one's permission, with all its faults, left entirely on its own to fend for itself when you are dead and gone, and no one will help it, correct your bad grammar . . . and then, goodness knows how, without you and utterly alone, it will gradually begin to gain strength, aided less by all the pains you took than by your mistakes and omissions, and will spread its wings in the grave and, forgetting and repudiating you (what use are *you*?) will set out, hundred-mouthed, to live its destined life as a book.[6]

Or here is Franz Kafka, a "Western" example: Kafka left his works to the mercy of fate, and yet is famous today no less than Nabokov.

I once shared these thoughts with a friend who was studying Kafka. She was impatient with me: "You can write all you want, but you are neither Kafka, nor Nabokov!"

Despite all my many years here, as hard as I've tried to retrain my "circular" Russian brain into an orderly, more "linear" thinking, I am still amazed (and at times annoyed) by the Anglo-Saxon—American linguistic habit of taking words more literally—at face value—than the inexact and inferential Russians do. "The notions of 'idle talk,' 'superfluities,' and 'vain ostentation,' all of which designated to the Puritans irrational, aimless . . . behaviors. . . . Hence, dispassionate instrumentalism was given a decisive upper hand over and against every application of artistic tendencies."[7]

Compare this with Tertz's definition of the Russian character as fluid and amorphous, thinking and living artistically, unable to manage the very serious practical side of daily life,[8] "ready to wear the first aspect that comes along, whether coarse or delicate, otherworldly or brutish, but always lacking precision."[9] Based on communal rituals rather than on the rational structure of rules—rituals unlike societal protocols are more concerned with the idea of a rule rather than a rule itself—Russian words and concepts generously allow for less precision, more approximation, and many tacit and contingent meanings: "Knowing nothing about someone or something we often form a notion of it according to a verbal image, the color and fragrance of the name."[10]

In contrast to its Western counterpart Russian is a "high-context," hypothetical culture: "We Russians still look and act like travelers. No one has a defined sphere of engagement; we have no rules for anything; we don't even have a home. Nothing that can tie us up . . . nothing durable, nothing permanent; everything flows by, goes by, without leaving a print either within or outside us," noted Pyotr Chaadaev in his *Philosophical Letters* (1831).[11]

A century later Abram Tertz made a similar observation about the striking lack of Russian sculptural art—which requires an awareness of form. Instead Russia makes up for the lack of it by songs and paintings—something that flows: "In the same order of things, there is our violation of the hierarchy of genres . . . our constant disagreements with strictly literary frames of reference, our failure to produce stories with a strong plot, the amorphousness of our prose and drama, the spiritual overcharging of our speech."[12]

Anyway, I'm a fan of Kafka, but it doesn't mean I intend to imitate him. Call me a Russian, but occasionally I bristle at the local tendency to see things in terms of contest and competition, binary oppositions and role models. Every so often some of my American friends tend to gallingly settle for simplified, clear-cut formulas like "Postcommunist Russia is the next America," "Joseph Brodsky is the successor of Nabokov":[13] it's as if Russia or Brodsky don't have any significance outside the context of generally accepted standards of greatness. This type of "literalism" aggravated Nabokov's Russianness as well.[14] He called such narrow understanding of concepts a *poshlost,* or vulgarity, that often takes on a form of political correctness: "*Poshlost* speaks in such concepts as 'America is no better than Russia' or 'We all share in Germany's guilt'" (*SO,* I#7, 101).

However, sharing Nabokov's contempt for literalism, I was faulting him for being an occasional victim of his own pedantry. Lamenting the loss of his blooming linguistic springtime in the Russian *Lolita,* he couldn't help but grumble elsewhere: "A very bothersome feature that Russian presents is the dearth, vagueness, and clumsiness of technical terms. For example, the simple phrase 'to park a car' comes out—if translated back from the Russian—as 'to leave an automobile standing for a long time'" (*SO,* I#3, 35–36).

What nonsense! How pedestrian it is to describe car parking when we can blissfully recite from memory:

And what Russian does not love fast driving? How could his soul, which is so eager to whirl round and round, to forget everything in a mad carouse, to exclaim sometimes, "To hell with it all!"? . . . Oh, you *troika,* you bird of *troika,* who invented you? You could only have been born among a high-spirited people in a land that does not like doing things by halves . . . And the *troika* dashes on and on! . . . Is it not like that that you, too, Russia, are speeding along like spirited *troika* that nothing can overtake?[15]

Why park or drive at all when we can fly? I will never read him again!

In his *Lectures on Literature,* Nabokov—the entomologist, kindly ruler in his kingdom of butterflies and insects—touchingly conveys the suffering of Gregor Samsa, transformed into a beetle in Kafka's *Metamorphosis.* He keenly feels how agonizing it is for Gregor—now a six-legged insect—to stand on his "third pair" of legs, still picturing them as a "second pair"—that is, as human legs. . . . But then: "Curiously enough," Nabokov enlightens his readers, "Gregor the beetle never found out that he had wings under the hard covering of his back. (This is a very nice observation on my part to be treasured all your lives. Some Gregors, some Joes and Janes, do not know that they have wings.)" (*LOL,* 259).

Nabokov's sympathy is natural: we can all understand the frustration of not being able to merge with a world that has turned its back on us. And yet, aware of the earthbound insect's pain, he nonetheless impassively uses Gregor's winglessness—his desire to fit back into humanity instead of proudly flying away as an insect—to make an instructive, a superior, such a practical Nabokovian point. Very insensitive. . . . The "true" Russian writer would have spent pages and pages agonizing over Gregor's miserable fate as if it were his own.

To Nabokov's heartlessness, to his obscure Russianness buried so deep one could go mad trying to find it, I preferred Goncharov, Gogol, and Tertz—even the sarcastic Dr. Chekhov. With them it was far more comfortable, kinder, gentler. But even then, already having put aside my half-read *Lolita,* Nabokov—*Nabokov himself,* in all his frosty majesty—was to give me no peace.

In 1999, to mark the hundredth anniversary of the former compatriot's birth, Moscow's *Nezavisimaya Gazeta* asked me to review the exhibition "Nabokov under Glass" then at the New York Public Library. What struck me most at the exhibition was Nabokov's notebooks. I returned again and again to look at them as I walked around the hall.

These notebooks drew me in—to see, to verify, to leave no doubt: it can't be—Nabokov is me!—I thought. His notes were my own. Not the contents—surely, I'm no Nabokov—but the phrases, beginning in English and continuing in Russian and vice versa. He was right to say, "I don't believe that people think in languages" (*SO,* I#2, 14), they think "in images, and now and then a Russian phrase or an English phrase will form with the foam of the brainwave" (ibid.). Snatches of words, snatches of thoughts— in whatever language the writing comes out . . .

Those who live in several languages know, and at times can almost sense, how their minds wander not between words but between worlds. And you yourself can't say why and how they alternate. Nabokov is me!

NABOKOV UNDER GLASS

The 1999 centenary exhibition "Nabokov under Glass" presented archival materials brought in 1991 from Montreux, where Nabokov lived from 1961 to his death in 1977.

Apart from first editions of Nabokov's books and correspondence with his wife Véra, translators, publishers, and friends, the most—to my mind—daunting display was two books opened to their tables of contents: *55 Short Stories from the New Yorker 1949* and *The Best American Short Stories*. Everything was as it should be: the name of the author, the name of the story, the page number. . . . And beside them, grades penciled in: B, C, D. In the *New Yorker* anthology only two authors got A's (A pluses in fact): Nabokov himself for the story "Collette," which later became a chapter in *Speak, Memory* and *Drugie berega*, and J. D. Salinger for "A Perfect Day for Bananafish." In the anthology of the best American short stories, Nabokov was less generous with his praise: just one A, for Nabokov's own "Time and Ebb." Most of the others got D's, C's at best.

In a 1964 interview with *Playboy*, to the question "What do you want to accomplish or leave behind—or should this be of no concern to the writer?" Nabokov replied:

> Well, in the matter of accomplishment, of course, I don't have a 35-year plan or program, but I have fair inkling of my literary afterlife. I have sensed certain hints, I have felt the breeze of certain promises. No doubt there will be ups and downs, long periods of slump. With the Devil's connivance, I open a newspaper of 2063 and in some article on the books page I find: "Nobody reads Nabokov or Fulmerford today." Awful question: Who is this unfortunate Fulmerford? (*SO*, I#3, 34)

My usual trouble with Nabokov is not that he's vain and peremptory. After all, Pushkin knew his own worth too. The difference is that Nabokov didn't pay for the privilege of comprehending his gift, for insight that altered the balance between humanity and nature. Pushkin paid: "the lot of the poet was repaid by adversities in everyday life."[16] They laughed at him, didn't take him seriously. Even his death looked like a joke: his bullet struck d'Anthès's button, and d'Anthès shot him dead. "Fate has a sense of humor." Old Tolstoy ran away from home and died a miserable death in some obscure train station. Gogol was buried alive, in a trance, screaming for some mystical ladder to heaven.

But Nabokov got away with it. Fate spared him from ridicule (or perhaps refused him this favor?). Not an American himself, Nabokov had a stellar career in American letters. Written by a Russian émigré from Europe, *Lolita* is now an American classic. He taught at Cornell. He published in prestigious journals. He's been translated the world over . . . Emigration was good to the author. He once declared America "a second home in the true sense of the word" (*SO*, I#2, 10).

Real emigrants (especially Russian, that is, communally conscious emigrants) are supposed to suffer from their expatriation solitude. Good emigrants run back home at the first opportunity, as did another well-known exile of ours, Alexander Isaevich Solzhenitsyn. But Nabokov made his exile a home, and to spite fate found happiness here. (Even if he only pretended, what a brilliant deception it was!) In short, he didn't clear his debt for talent and fame with suffering.

So one might have left the exhibition—bitter about the D's and the noisome index cards of things Nabokov hated the most: "I hate four Doctors: Dr. Freud, Dr. Zhivago, Dr. Schweitzer, and Dr. Castro." Again he's displeased with someone!

On the way out one would have noted that Nabokov's obedient wife carried on all the business correspondence regarding translations of his Russian books. The letters made us think of scenes from Stacy Schiff's excellent biography of Véra: Nabokov's brusque manner with his wife around students; her wiping the blackboard after her husband's lectures because he thought it beneath him; taking his notes; grading his tests; sharpening his pencils; writing his letters; driving him everywhere . . . [17]

And that's how I would have left the exhibition, forever outraged by the writer's personality—if not for one thing: the display of his notebooks near the exit.

More than the other memorabilia, these scribbled notes were a testament to the uniqueness of the American Nabokov: he never touched a typewriter; he couldn't work the technology of a country where Bulgakov's famous Russian formula for totalitarianism, "No documents, no person," [18] had been replaced by the American utilitarian creed, "No machine, no person."

No matter how American the English-writing Nabokov may have appeared to his readers, his polyglot notes betray him as a traditional intellectual in a Chekhovian mold—a talented Russian aristocrat who simply adjusted better than many others, who made himself adapt to other shores; who learnt to change his stripes to suit the moment or the mood: today Russian, tomorrow European, and American the next day.

From a 1962 interview with the BBC (*SO*, I#2, 13):

Do you still feel Russian, in spite of so many years in America?

I do feel Russian and I think that my Russian works . . . that I have written during these years, are a kind of tribute to Russia.

From a 1966 interview with the *Paris Review* (*SO*, I#7, 98):

Do you consider yourself an American?

Yes, I do. I am as American as April in Arizona.

From a 1971 interview with the *Bayerische Rundfunk* (*SO*, I#19, 192):

I see myself as an American writer raised in Russia, educated in England, imbued with the culture of Western Europe.[19]

And finally—"Nobody can decide if I am a middle-aged American writer or an old Russian writer—or an ageless international freak" (*SO*, I#7, 106)—here's the modern "combinational talent" (ibid., I#2, 15), the hallmark of the protean present-day hero, a free man in an open spatio-temporal and semiotic field: he can be anyone, write about anything, in any language. He can travel to any physical or artistic time and space (with the natural exception of Soviet-totalitarian territory).

The polyglot self of the notebooks showed how Nabokov invented himself as American (for example, in *Lolita*), accepted his Russianness in *Speak, Memory*, and so became an international celebrity.

A learned academic might say there's nothing special about the multilingual Russian aristocrat: Pushkin wrote in two languages, Nabokov's own parents (and their children) lived in three—Russian, English, and French, as does Nabokov's son Dmitri (and apparently in Italian as well) . . .

But there's a difference. For Pushkin and Nabokov's noble forebears, the native land with its defined places and addresses marked the borders of home. For Nabokov in emigration, home meant the very absence of those addresses and borders. Pushkin and the Nabokovs had their homeland, but Nabokov had to console himself with the notion that "One is always at home in one's past."

Vladimir Nabokov belongs to a lonely but numerous class (the incomparable Nabokov, who even as a schoolboy "was intensely averse to joining movements or associations of any kind" [*SM*, 143], will have to forgive me for seeing him as "typical," as part of the whole) of emigrants, exiles, *étrangers*, expatriates, voluntary and involuntary, past and future, who speak, write, and think in all languages simultaneously as a result not of cultural tradition or circumstances of birth but rather of the vicissitudes of fate:

> Water in Turkish is "su," said Pnin, a linguist by necessity, and went on with his fascinating past: Completed university education in Prague. Was connected with various scientific institutions. Then——"Well, to make a long story very short: habitated in Paris from 1925, abandoned France at beginning of Hitler war. Is now here. Is American citizen." (*Pnin*, 383)

Centuries of exile literature, from the Italian Francesco Petrarch to the American James Baldwin to the Russian Joseph Brodsky, confirm the necessity of overcoming an expatriate international solitude by embracing linguistic challenges. Emigrants have to choose a tongue, be it native or newly adopted, for creating a better, happier, more stable reality they can now make into a home.

For many multilinguals, like Pnin, the native language is a snail shell in which to hide from their newfound, yet unfamiliar abode: "If his Russian was music, his English was murder" (*Pnin*, 409–10). Those exiles turn to their primary tongue, the only treasure not taken from them at the border: it can't be stolen, lost, or destroyed. But there are others, like Nabokov (and his kind are few), for whom the new language, free of the limits of the old, opens new creative horizons:

It had taken me some forty years to invent Russia and Western Europe, and now I was faced by the task of inventing America. . . . Considerations of depth and perspective (a suburban lawn, a mountain meadow) led me to build a number of North American sets. . . . I chose American motels instead of Swiss hotels or English inns only because I am trying to be an American writer and claim only the same rights that other American writers enjoy. . . . All my Russian readers know that my old worlds—Russian, British, German, French—are just as fantastic and personal as my new one is. (*Lolita*, 312, 315)

Beyond the borders, in a different dimension, carried beyond the margins of the routine, you don't have anything familiar at hand—no yardstick by which to measure this new life's unknowns. You have only yourself and your language; words, past or present, by which to make your lonely world inhabitable. The exile creates "his own mirage, which becomes a new *mir* [world] . . . by the very act of his shedding, as it were, the age he lives in" (*SO*, I#8, 112).

The process of creating, whether it's in the new language or in the old, enables the exile to return home at any point, to travel between several worlds, translating and inventing himself en route. It's not just a question of mastering a new grammar and vocabulary but of creating one's own artistic tongue—"an individual vital dialect [individualnoe krovnoe narechie]" (*DB*, 133).

Nabokov may have been particularly sympathetic to Gregor

Samsa's confusion (save for the didactic tone) because Gregor's exile was so particularly hopeless. Cut off from the familiar habits of his human past, imprisoned in the foreign body of an insect, Gregor can't find the wings—of language, of art, of new life.

From the prison camp of Dubrovlag, Tertz described his dislocation in similar terms—as paralyzing bewilderment: "life, which seemed so incredibly stable in its repetitiveness, suddenly reveals itself as unpredictable and liable to dissolve in a myriad chance events of the smallest kind."[20]

Even for the "Western" Nabokov, life abroad at Cambridge "began on a note of embarrassment, a note that was to recur rather persistently during three years of residence" (*SM*, 202).

His own creation Timofey Pnin, who fled the prison house of socialism for America's freedom, experienced the same shock of dislocation:

He was . . . too wary, too persistently on the lookout for diabolical pitfalls, too painfully on the alert lest his erratic surroundings (unpredictable America) inveigle him into some bit of preposterous oversight. It was the world that was absent-minded and it was Pnin whose business it was to set it straight. His life was a constant war with insensate objects that fell apart, or attacked him, or refused to function, or viciously got themselves lost as soon as they entered the sphere of his existence. . . . A special danger area in Pnin's case was the English language. (*Pnin*, 367)

"On the other hand," Nabokov reassures us in his notes on *The Metamorphosis,* "the isolation, and the strangeness, of so-called reality—this is, after all, something which constantly characterizes the artist, the genius, the discoverer" (*LOL,* 260). (A constructive thought—if only the pathetic Gregor Samsa could have benefited from this encouraging assertion.)

To be sure, without the solitude of exile (whatever shape it may take—from entomologist to writer, from aristocrat to penniless poet, from man to insect, from present to past, from past to future) the creative act is impossible. It's the fruit of suffering and its salvation at the same time. . . . If only one's strength holds out!

"The history of man is the history of pain!" (*Pnin,* 493), Timofey Pnin once pronounced with stoic resignation.

Tertz was protected from this pain at Dubrovlag by that which was dear to him: world literature and letters to his wife— "I often sit down to a letter not because I intend writing anything of importance to you, but just to touch a piece of paper which you will be holding in your hand."[21]

Pushkin's poetry, Volume 18 of the "Soviet Gold Fund of Literature" (*Pnin,* 409) and the aspiration to "writing a *Petite Histoire* of Russian culture, in which a choice of Russian Curiosities, Customs, Literary Anecdotes, and so forth would be presented in such a way as to reflect in miniature *la Grande Histoire*—Major Concatenations of Events" (ibid., 418), saved Pnin at Waindell College.

And in Berlin and Paris, at Cambridge and Cornell, Nabokov was rescued by his own art: "The writer's art is his real passport" (*SO*, I#6, 63).

Human history isn't just a history of pain, it's a history of the courage to prevail.

THE KEY TO OTHER SHORES

In works of literature the real clash happens not between the characters
of the novel but between the author and the reader.
—Vladimir Nabokov, *Drugie berega*

In my quest for metaphysical justice I may have been unfairly hard on Nabokov, setting the price of artistic good fortune— human misfortune—too high.[22] Not in vain he admitted in *Speak, Memory*, "The story of my college years in England is really the story of my trying to become a Russian writer" (203). If Nabokov didn't find his Russianness until he'd left Russia, he lost his nation long before he discovered his nationality. By this loss, perhaps, un- like other national greats—Pushkin, Gogol, Tolstoy—he paid for his talent *before* he achieved fame, *not after.*

We may recall the illustrious chronophobiac's account at the beginning of *Speak, Memory* and *Drugie berega.* Though "common sense tells us that our existence is but a brief crack of light between two eternities of darkness. . . . I know, however, of a young chrono- phobiac who experienced something like panic when looking for the first time at homemade movies that had been taken a few weeks before his birth" (*SM*, 9).

Let's assume this young chronophobiac is Nabokov himself, different from others even then; not like the rest of us who view "the prenatal abyss with more calm than the one [we are] heading for" (*SM*, 9).

On the contrary:

> He saw a world that was practically unchanged—the same house, the same people—and then realized that he did not exist there at all and that nobody mourned his absence. He caught a glimpse of his mother waving from an upstairs window, and that unfamiliar gesture disturbed him, as if it were some mysterious farewell. But what particularly frightened him was the sight of a brand-new baby carriage standing there on the porch, with the smug, encroaching air of a coffin; even that was empty, as if, in the reverse course of events, his very bones had disintegrated. (*SM*, 9)

The self-assured chronophobiac is certain that life won't go on without him after his death. His books and his heroes will preserve him for posterity. But *before* birth. . . . What if he'd never been born? Only the fact of his nativity guarantees the writer's posthumous existence.

Michael Wood has described Nabokov's predicament: "Children and books are marks to be left on the world without us, the world of our death; death can't be defeated but it can be accused, compromised. But if the first pram were never filled, there would be no children or books or anything else; and books at least can be seen as desperate attempts to cover up this most alarming of all possibilities."[23]

Wood's comments echo the writer's own conviction that death by expatriation—a loss of one's native country—is unbearable in just one instance: "Exile means to an artist only one thing—the banning of his books" (*SO*, I#9, 118). And though Nabokov pretends indifference to his situation—immediately adding "It's Russia's loss, not mine" (ibid.)—there's no mistaking his desire to break through the walls of time to conquer nonexistence (eventually these efforts should also permit him to overcome the spatial [not only temporal] boundaries of his lost *rodina* [native land]):

> Over and over again, my mind has made colossal efforts to distinguish the faintest of personal glimmers in the impersonal darkness on both sides of my life. That this darkness is caused merely by the walls of time separating me and my bruised fists from the free world of timelessness is a belief I gladly share with the most gaudily painted savage. (*SM*, 9–10)

World literary history has shown more than once how these "walls of time" can be retrospectively overcome: in Russia, Pushkin, Gogol, Tolstoy, and Dostoevsky ultimately became the Pushkin, Gogol, Tolstoy, and Dostoevsky of their biographers. But Nabokov, especially the Nabokov of *Speak, Memory*, was able to position himself in a world in which the time after the fact is as significant as the time before the fact.

The memoirs contain a sixteenth chapter, "On *Conclusive Evidence*,"[24] in which an invented critic writes a pseudo-review explaining that the events in Nabokov's book are "seen to fall into the pattern of predicted loss, of pathetic attempts to retain the doomed, the departing, the lovely dying things of a life that was trying, rather desperately, to think of itself in terms of future retrospective" (OCE, 253).

Literary scholars will point out that it's not so unusual for a writer to see his life in terms of "future retrospective," or at any rate to foretell it in his works. Take Pushkin for instance:

> Death in a duel so suited him that it looked like a passage from one of Pushkin's works. The passage, it's true, came out as something of a parody, but after all that was also in his style. . . . Didn't he have a presentiment of this concluding stunt in *The Stone Guest*, in "The Shot," in "The Queen of Spades"? Or do we see in action here the ancient literary convention according to which fate mysteriously makes short work of an author, using the texts of his works as a blueprint?[25]

But if Pushkin prophetically foretold his fate, then Nabokov told his backwards. Making sense of the present and future requires continuity with the past. Emigration painfully ruptured that continuity—life had to start anew. Time was broken—things and concepts familiar from before were no longer part of the current reality. So to create a meaningful past, Nabokov had to project artistic patterns of significance upon it retrospectively. He regarded exile as a theme of "'intrinsic loss' running through the whole book" (OCE, 250), as the riddle of his subsequent life and his search for extratemporal answers.

Of his mother, Nabokov writes:

> As if feeling that in a few years the tangible part of her world would perish, she cultivated an extraordinary consciousness of the various time marks distributed throughout our country place. She cherished her own past with the same retrospective fervor I now do her image and my past. Thus, in a way, I inherited an exquisite simulacrum— the beauty of intangible property, unreal estate—and this proved a splendid training for the endurance of later losses. (*SM*, 25–26)

"Anyone can create the future but only a wise man can create the past" (*BS*, 10) reflects the philosopher Adam Krug, in *Bend Sinister* doomed to a fate even worse than his author's in emigration: before madness eclipses his mind Krug is forced to rely on his own wits to overcome the mad nightmare of life in totalitarian Padukgrad. The narrator of the story "Lance" (1952) reiterates Krug's comment: "The future is but the obsolete in reverse."[26]

Having himself once lost a life, having then created it anew through his books and heroes in a different language, Nabokov had good reason to make the following grandiose pronouncement: "I do not believe in time" (*SM*, 106). Playing his own critic in "On *Conclusive Evidence,*" he explains that the author of the memoirs had experienced all the pain and appeal of nostalgia long before the 1917 Bolshevik Revolution wrecked the milieu of his childhood and youth.

Nabokov later said that even his books he plans in "future retrospective":

> In professional action I look forward, rather than back, as I try to foresee the evolution of the work in progress, try to perceive the fair copy in the crystal of my inkstand, try to read the proof, long before it is printed, by projecting into an imagined section of time the growth of the book, whose every line belongs to the present moment, which in its turn is nothing but the ever rising horizon of the past. (*SO*, I#14, 155)

Perhaps Nabokov's greatest achievement was indeed the transformation of his ruined past into artistic triumph. As he wrote of the postrevolutionary Russian émigré poet Vladislav Khodasevich—likely with his own self in mind: "Even genius does not save one in Russia; in exile, one is saved by genius alone" (*SO*, A#1, 224). As the examples of Tertz and Pnin or the unfortunate case of Gregor Samsa have demonstrated, only in creative activity can the exile find salvation.

The pseudo-critic helps define the exiled Nabokov genius, noting that the "permanent importance" of his memoirs "lies in its being the meeting point of an impersonal art form and a very personal life story" (OCE, 248). Of course, all reminiscences, memoirs, or autobiographies combine an impersonal form with a personal history. But an immortal masterpiece differs from a rambling tell-all tale in the degree of talent that confers artistic significance on an always personally significant life story: "The best part of a writer's biography is not the record of his adventures but the story of his style" (*SO*, I#14, 154–55).

It is, in fact, the author's style that determines the readers' interest and, accordingly, our reception of this "very personal life story" as a work of art. The better the writer, the more engrossing (and the more difficult) is the reader's search for the genuine (that is to say, the creative) key to his style. As Nabokov himself advised, "A good reader is bound to make fierce efforts when wrestling with a difficult author, but those efforts can be most rewarding after the bright dust has settled" (*SO*, I#18, 183).

In an attempt to "wrestle" with my "difficult author" I quote the aphorism of the anticzarist revolutionary humanist Vladimir Korolenko, well known to every civic-minded Russian: "Man is born to be happy, as a bird is born to fly."[27] Nabokov satirically reused this line in *Bend Sinister:* "I shall always remember . . . what he [Padukgrad's dictator Paduk] said that time they arrested him at the big meeting in the Godeon: 'I,' he said, 'am born to lead as naturally as a bird flies.' I think it is the greatest thought ever expressed in human language, and the most poetical one. Name me the writer who has said anything approaching it?" (*BS*, 18). I quote Korolenko because Nabokov, while opposing popular revolutions and general happiness, *should have* taken these particular words of Korolenko to heart despite their ideological differences. Of all people, Nabokov truly was born for happiness, the young lord of a Russian estate and the product of a "cosmopolitan childhood" (*SM*, 184).

"I was a difficult and stubborn child, spoiled to a wonderful extreme (spoil your children as much as you can, ladies and gentlemen, you don't know what awaits them!)" (*DB*, 179).

We really don't know. The West (especially America with its absolute belief in the great equalizing powers of democracy), has lived by a different truth: everyone is born equal and makes his own individual way in his own free-choice–based pursuit of happiness. Though he lacked faith in Russian, communal egalitarianism, the protean, combinational Nabokov committed himself to its Western individualistic type long before his American years. Its appeal lay in the possibility of an inventive, bootstrap aristocratism when a hereditary one had ceased to exist.

Witold Gombrowicz, the famed Polish writer forced into emigration at the beginning of World War II, describes the artist-in-exile's strange elect status: "An artist in emigration, however, is forced to exist not only outside of his people, but also outside of the elite. . . . He is like a bankrupt count who sees that the manners of the salon are worthless if there is no salon. . . . We have to find a way to feel like aristocrats once again (in the deeper sense of the word)."[28]

Nabokov was this very same "bankrupt count," searching for a new shire, a new salon, an ancestral home in an alien land.

In the attempt to regain this ancestral home, it's not uncommon for emigrants (perhaps of all nations—not only the Russians, and not only the self-assured ones like Nabokov) to treat the countries sheltering them with superiority, distrust, even spite. By regarding the natives as specters, as strangers in their own land, by assigning themselves superior status, emigrants reclaim the lost relevance of their once existing places:

> As I look back at those years of exile, I see myself, and thousands of other Russians, leading an odd but by no means unpleasant existence, in material indigence and intellectual luxury, among perfectly unimportant strangers, spectral Germans and Frenchmen in whose more or less illusory cities, we, émigrés, happened to dwell. These aborigines were to the mind's eye as flat and transparent as figures cut out of cellophane, and although we used their gadgets, applauded their clowns, picked their roadside plums and apples, no real communication, of the rich human sort so widespread in our own midst, existed between us and them. . . . in the course of almost one-fifth of a century spent in Western Europe I have not had, among

the sprinkling of Germans and Frenchmen I knew . . .
more than two good friends all told. (*SM*, 215–17)

In *The Gift* Fyodor Godunov-Cherdyntsev spends an entire
tramcar trip (and Nabokov an entire printed page) threading "the
points of his biased indictment" (*G*, 82) against an unsuspecting
Berliner, his fellow passenger. These points mean to account for
"the Russian conviction that the German is in small numbers vulgar and in large numbers—unbearably vulgar" (ibid., 81). In the
same breath, Fyodor tries to assure himself that this is "a conviction unworthy of an artist" (ibid.).

To prove that this belief is "unworthy," the narrator ultimately
reveals the Berliner who evokes Fyodor's anti-German sentiments
to be a Russian. Yet Nabokov himself never hesitated to point out
vulgarity in others, and not only in the native residents of "the
spectral world through which we serenely paraded our sores and
our arts" (*SM*, 216). While Germany, in particular, had always remained a locus of vulgarity for him,[29] he was no more favorably
disposed towards his fellow Russians: "Not many of my compatriots and fellow writers evoked in me feelings of personal comfort"
(*DB*, 287).

Carefully read his memoirs and novels, and you'll encounter
the following kind of boasting more than once: "There existed in
Russia . . . a special type of school-age boy who . . . excels quite
phenomenally at soccer and chess, and learns with the utmost ease
and grace any kind of sport or game of skill. . . . I was a good

skater on ice. . . . Very quickly I learned two or three tricky steps on the wooden floor of the rink and in no ballroom have I danced with more zest or ability" (*SM*, 159–60).

In *Drugie berega,* Nabokov's assertion of his special kind is even more resolute: "I belonged to their [those school-age boys'] breed" (*DB*, 251).

Of course he did! Do we dare to doubt?

This breed of boys believed the world revolved around them and felt surprised and upset whenever they weren't the center of attention. When he learned after many years that his private teachers of English (Burness) and drawing (Cummings) had lives that extended beyond the walls of the Nabokov household, the writer was taken aback: "When I learned these later developments, I experienced a queer shock; it was as if life had impinged upon my creative rights by wriggling on beyond the subjective limits so elegantly and economically set by childhood memories that I thought I had signed and sealed" (*SM*, 69).

Nabokov never stopped drawing the whole world into his personal "subjective limits." Visiting Cambridge after seventeen years away, he dropped in on his former acquaintance Nesbit: "An accidental worry (the cousin or maiden sister who kept house for him had just been removed to Binet's clinic or something) seemed to prevent him from concentrating on the very personal and urgent matter I wanted to speak to him about" (*SM*, 212).

Nabokov's a great man, no argument. But this is simply rude. Imagine being friends with a person who is annoyed with you just because you dared to trouble over your own *accidental* affairs—a close relative's illness—when he has deigned to share with you his *important* ones.

But that's what makes Nabokov Nabokov—*Solus Rex.*[30] What does he need friends for? He was born first (and not among equals), the axis around which everyone else's life revolves. He is so central, in fact, that when all is said and done only he and Véra, the sole addressee of all his books, populate the pages of the memoirs: "The years are passing, my dear, and presently nobody will know what you and I know" (*SM*, 231). With these words he drives away the readers, who were to serve only as intermediary witnesses to the author's recollections.

Did Nabokov really need these readers at all? He assured us that "an artist should [not] bother about his audience. His best audience is the person he sees in his shaving mirror every morning" (*SO*, I#2, 18). Deprived of his Russian audience by the Soviet regime, Nabokov would claim that "I grew less and less interested in Russia and more and more indifferent to the once-harrowing thought that my books would remain banned there as long as my contempt for the police state and political oppression prevented me from entertaining the vaguest thought of return" (ibid., I#3, 37).

Granted he couldn't have a Russian audience, but he certainly had an English-speaking one. Some critics suggest that Nabokov didn't mean to drive his readers away from the pages of the book. The "you" and "I" of the memoirs simply represent a literary device; they signify "the intimacy of a text, of reading: we can share the couple's feelings only if we don't invade them."[31]

Fine, but why do even his artistic devices, his rhetoric—those "pieces of a performance"[32]—have to be so disdainful and discourteous towards everybody—any audience, any reader? Besides, as a professor, he was obliged to have American audiences anyway. Asked once whether teaching had taught him anything important, Nabokov replied without a hint of discomfiture:

> My method of teaching precluded genuine contact with my students. At best, they regurgitated a few bits of my brain during examinations. Every lecture I delivered had been carefully, lovingly handwritten and typed out [by Véra of course!], and I leisurely read it out in class. . . . Vainly I tried to replace my appearances at the lectern by taped records to be played over the college radio. (*SO,* I#7, 104)

He encompassed the whole world within his personal subjective limits. He slammed the door shut on readers (both Russian and American) of his autobiography, preferring the company of Véra, his devoted alter ego. He deprived his poor students of the contact they deserved, shooing them away from his literary relations with other writers.

German "aborigines" and Russian "compatriots," students and readers, teachers and colleagues—they all shared the fate of the peasant girl Polenka, who in the young master's life "was the first to have the poignant power . . . of burning a hole in my sleep and jolting me into clammy consciousness, whenever I dreamed of her" (*SM*, 163). "Although in real life," Nabokov unabashedly relates, "I was even more afraid of being revolted by her dirt-caked feet and stale-smelling clothes than of insulting her by the triteness of quasi-seigniorial advances" (ibid., 163–64).

Here the "unique" author gives in to the no less trite snobbishness and squeamishness that he claims he always tries to escape. And note, sounding very much the serf owner, Godunov-Cherdyntsev—one of Nabokov's favorite characters—praises his father's "special easy knack he showed in dealing with a horse, a dog, a gun, a bird, or a peasant boy"[33] (*G*, 113).

What an interesting semantic sequence!

And while it may be historically accurate, the following statement of Nabokov's own rings false: "Belonging, as he did by choice, to the great classless intelligentsia of Russia, my father thought it right to have me attend a school that was distinguished by its democratic principles, its policy of nondiscrimination in matters of rank, race, and creed, and its up-to-date educational methods" (*SM*, 143).

Despite the absence of class differences at school, we discover that Nabokov was an island unto himself: "I didn't give school a morsel of my soul, saving it all for my home pleasures—*my own* games, *my own* hobbies and fancies, *my* butterflies, *my* favorite books" (*DB*, 241). He, in fact, ridiculed his teachers for their efforts to uphold the school's democratic principles: "another thing that provoked resentment was my driving to and from school in an automobile and not traveling by streetcar or horsecab as the other boys, good little democrats, did" (*SM*, 143).

If noblesse oblige is the mark of the true aristocrat, then Nabokov should be making no claim to primacy. He's seemed only a bit better than the self-indulgent masters of Chekhov's *The Cherry Orchard*,[34] who heartlessly forgot their old servant Firs in the boarded-up house.

Like the peasant boy and Polenka with her dirty feet, none of us are worthy of his greatness. Affinities of birth or intellect count for nothing. We're all commoners, equally unworthy. Nabokov is the *Solus Rex* in glacial solitude, the lonely genius and proud aristocrat who never learned democracy, despite a progressive education, the example of a liberal father, and twenty years in classless America, which he called home.

But here, I believe, we have the secret of Nabokov's American (read, "world") success. As it happens, despite his exclusiveness, his self-image as *Solus Rex*, Nabokov was kin to American democratic "self-made man" individualism after all.

Max Weber assures us that "*Individual* motives and personal self-interests [in America] were . . . placed in the service of maintaining and propagating the 'middle class' Puritan ethic, with all its ramifications. . . . To repeat, it is not the ethical *doctrine* of a religion, but that form of ethical conduct upon which *premiums* are placed that matters."[35] This ethic—the tradition of hard, methodical work, the results of which proved one's status as the elect, mixed with a rational way of life—explains the writer's great triumph in establishing his new sovereignty, his new salon, on American soil. He got on brilliantly in this Weber-defined lonely, self-absorbed, dispassionate though classless, land because Tocqueville's concept of American democratic individualism, a bulwark against the pressures of society and the crowd,[36] was instilled in him from childhood. He combined the old aristocratism of the hereditary *Solus Rex* with the new, self-driven American character, helped by God only because he is able to help himself, thus creating the Nabokov we know today: the self-enhanced *Solus Rex*. After all, "in America, the old tradition respected the self-made man more than the heir."[37]

Nabokov was right in seeing that he wouldn't have become a writer had he remained in Russia: "It is not improbable that had there been no revolution in Russia, I would have devoted myself entirely to lepidopterology and never written any novels at all" (*SO*, I#7, 100).

Compassionate, traditional, mythical, emotional, communal, stagnant, slothful Russia, steeped in Pushkin, Gogol, Bulgakov, and Oblomov—illiberal, autocratic, or socialist class society though it may have been—simply didn't care for the individualistic author at the time. Bright, talented Sirin, the future Nabokov, felt and foresaw it even then. So he solitarily stared in his shaving mirror for a time, disregarding all other readers except himself, insisting in the words of Godunov-Cherdyntsev: "The real writer should ignore all readers but one, that of the future, who in his turn is merely the author reflected in time" (*G*, 340).

And half a century later, when Nabokov no longer needed to shave at all, this future reader took shape in his native land. Nabokov is still read (although less in 2007 than in 2001) in the postcommunist Russia which has been agonizingly emerging from its "communalism"—a testimony to his wisdom. And yet these remaining post-1991 Russian readers have taken revenge on Nabokov—for the writer's conceit, coldness, and emphatic indifference to all us ordinary folks, unworthy of his genius; for his contempt of the Russian tradition of socially minded literature ("a work of art has no importance whatever to society" [*SO*, I#3, 33]). These readers have begun reading his books not only as art but also as books important to society, learning from them the hardest art of all—how to live for yourself, how to live on your own, and how to rely on yourself for happiness. These modern Russian readers, while gradually acquiring the traits of egoistic individualism that come with democracy, capitalism, and open borders, have followed Nabokov's own perception of art (ibid.)— "it is only important to the individual, and only the individual reader is important to me."

THREE

Poet, Genius, and Hero

NABOKOV AND PUSHKIN: WILL VERSUS FATE

Any personality could be repulsive if there is too much of it.
Overwhelming personality is always a hindrance,
even if it all consists of virtues, wit, and talent.
—Abram Tertz, *Mysli vrasplokh*

The carefree aristocrat, Pushkin, snug in his homeland, could afford the luxury of slickly rhyming *Volya* (freedom, will) with *Dolya* (fate, lot): "This world has no happiness, but there is peace and will. And long I've dreamed of lucky fate."[1] Nabokov had to rely on strength of will alone to "give to Mnemosyne [the muse of memory] not just the will, but the order [dat Mnemozine ne tolko volyu, no i zakon]" (*DB*, 133), a task for which responsible,

scrupulously measured prose was better suited than the frivolous
Pushkinian verse.

"If I try to rationalize them [my poems] I shall instantly lose
my ability to write them. You, I know, corrupted your poetry long
ago with words and meaning—and you will hardly continue writing verse now. You are too rich, too greedy. The Muse's charm lies
in her poverty" (*G*, 340–41), the poet Koncheyev instructs the
prose writer Godunov-Cherdyntsev, both alter egos of Vladimir
Nabokov.

Although Joseph Brodsky insisted that Nabokov, despite his
fame as a prose writer, "was in his own eyes primarily a poet" and
"wanted to prove to everyone that he was first and foremost a
poet,"[2] Brodsky's claim is entirely implausible: whoever this "everyone" may have been, he/she was ultimately not too important to
Nabokov as he chose to become an American writer, for publication mostly composing English prose, not Russian poetry. Although Nabokov did write poems in Russian it was more a matter
of his heart than his profession: to a question, "Which of the languages you speak do you consider the most beautiful," he replied,
"My head says, English, my heart, Russian. . . ." (*SO*, I#4, 49). Also
consider this rather prosaic and unambitious admission that when
he started writing English prose, his Russian verses "improve[d]
rather oddly in urgency and concentration" (ibid., I#3, 54).

While Nabokov believed that "in today's scientific classifications . . . the bamboo bridge between them [poetry and prose]
is the metaphor" (*SO*, I#3, 44), asserting that "the dividing line

between prose and poetry in some of the greatest English and American novels is not easy to draw" (*SO*, I#6, 64), he also observed that "Russian rhymes are incomparably more attractive and more abundant than English ones. No wonder a Russian prose writer frequents those beauties, especially in his youth" (ibid.). That is, he agreed that as there's a difference between languages—English and Russian—and countries—Russia and America—so there is a difference between their poetry and prose.

To develop further Koncheyev's thought, the "poverty" of "rich" rhymes in Russian poetry is the very secret of its charm; linguistically our artistic way of thinking fills the simplest of words with metaphor and color. What could be more trivial than rhyming *dolya* and *volya*, and what could be lovelier than this rhyme?

True art, in Tertz's definition, requires poverty—the absence of premeditated mastery and absolute artistic trust in this absence—as a precondition: "Art is always a more or less impromptu act of prayer. Try to catch hold of smoke."[3]

This is of course fine for the Russian hypothetical culture. But Nabokov aimed for international acclaim, and for smoke or prayers he had neither time nor hope. On other, unsympathetic shores he shelved forever not only his Russian language but also poetry as a vocation: "I am all for the ivory tower, and for writing to please one reader alone—one's own self. But one also needs some reverberation, if not response, and a moderate multiplication of one's self throughout a country or countries" (*SO*, I#3, 37). Poetry, we know, doesn't travel well (take *Onegin:* he's been waiting nearly two centuries for a rhyming translator, parallel to his great author); its lyrical voice is too weak to create an echo loud enough for the ambitious hero of *Speak, Memory*. (Even Joseph Brodsky, despite being well known as a poet, is still much better known not for his poetry but for his Nobel Prize and his prose essays.)

In an article on time in the works of Proust and Nabokov, Michael Wood analyzes the relations of both authors to chance and fate: "Proust believes in luck where Nabokov believes in effort."[4] The same formula could be applied to the art of Pushkin and Nabokov, explaining differences between versification—a free flight of images—and prose writing—semantics and style.

For Pushkin, versification was a magical, mysterious, divine gift, and it didn't matter how many drafts he went through before completing a masterpiece: grace, derived from trust in his poetic lot, "a sense of fellowship with fate, which liberated him from fear, suffering, and vanity,"[5] extended to his faith in his own blessed talent—as if with a wave of a magic wand he could transform Cinderella words like *dolya* and *volya* into captivating princess-rhymes.

Pushkin is a sorcerer, creator and a spectator of his own wonders. Upon the completion of the drama *Boris Godunov* (1825) he jubilantly wrote to his friend, the poet Pyotr Vyazemsky: "Ai, da Pushkin! Ai, da sukin syn!" (That Pushkin! That son of a bitch!). He was talking to himself then, not to Vyazemsky, and certainly not to us. Pushkin didn't have to worry about his reader, or to be concerned with the limits of his talent. He could allow himself to turn a blind eye to those limits, convinced that if he blundered—with simplicity, with repetition—the miracle of creation would cover up any poetic handicap: "A writer's word . . . can be of any kind he likes. It does not have to be figurative, precise, concrete, grammatically correct, or even literary. 'What an apt epithet!' is the cry of the gushing amateur. Absoluteness is the only criterion. Once uttered, a word should be absolute."[6]

The greatest motto of the unfettered, poetic Pushkin—"Obey thy God, and never mind, O Muse, the laurels or the stings"[7]—could never be shared by the prosaic Nabokov (although admittedly, his English translation of this particular poem is better than any other), who had suffered much from Russian artistic and impractical carelessness: in 1917 they destroyed his whole country in a creative zeal for building the romantic utopia of socialist brotherhood. He'd lost his past, and had little reason to trust in the goodwill of the future. So, to raise his own monument, to blaze "the nation's footpath to its site,"[8] for posterity, Nabokov had to strictly harness his muses and mirages.

Pushkin purposefully based his playful artistic faith on trust, superstition, and myth:

Pushkin professed trust in fate—a banal bit of wisdom—with as much conviction as if it were a guiding star that shone for him alone. In its light trust flares into a symbol of faith. . . . Pushkin was like a fish in water in the vicissitudes of fortune. . . . He played with fire every chance he got. . . . But even in the height of rage, he never tried to out-argue fate: he longed to experience its handshake.

That was the verification of his lot. He would go to a duel just as he threw himself under the fire of inspiration: impromptu, at every opportunity. He tempted fate in this thirst to be convinced that it remembered him. He was lucky. . . . But . . . the lot of the poet was repaid by adversities in everyday life. The sum was large and required compensation. The ancients called this the "jealousy of the gods."[9]

Nabokov, a Russian (albeit "an English child"), was probably no less superstitious. He often refers to the importance of fate in one's life. He confesses to being haunted by omens and acknowledges being "subject to the embarrassing qualms of superstition: a number, a dream, a coincidence can affect me obsessively— though not in the sense of absurd fears but as fabulous (and on the whole rather bracing) scientific enigmas incapable of being stated, let alone solved" (*SO*, I#16, 177). But he distrusts chance occurrences—superstitions should never interfere with life's order.

To the readers of Weber, who were brought up in the country of the Protestant work ethic, this sounds all too familiar: "There were . . . no magical means that would turn God's grace towards believers. . . . The resulting spiritual isolation of believers . . . provided the basis for Puritanism's absolutely negative position toward all aspects of culture and religion oriented to the sensuous and to *feelings*: they were useless for salvation and they promoted sentimental illusions and idolatrous superstition."[10]

Similarly, according to Nabokov, the aim of art is not to rely on fate, not to follow fortune's lead (ruthless chance can destroy even a solid aristocratic heritage), but to overcome it, to subject mortal fears, the qualms of superstition to rational, scientific explanation. Yet another Nabokov double (also "an English child" by virtue of his British mother), the writer Sebastian Knight in his own book *Success* analyzes human destiny, methodically classifying a great range of facts, which happen to determine the course of one's life.

Unlike Pushkin, Nabokov "out-argued," that is to say, rewrote, his *dolya* every step of the way. But he sensibly never dared to tempt it: his own life was far removed from madcaps, duels, and improvisations, showing a "disposition . . . to organize [his] life in a practical-rational manner."[11] In the words of the pseudo-critic from "On *Conclusive Evidence*," Nabokov "with his wife and son . . . lives happily . . . in the simple disguise of an obscure college professor of literature with spacious vacations devoted to butterfly hunting in the West" (OCE, 256–57). In an interview, Nabokov added: "As a private person, I happen to be good-natured, straightforward, plain-spoken, and intolerant of bogus art" (*SO*, I#15, 175).

Pushkin's tempestuous fate remains outside his poetry, outside inferior human motives, moves, and actions. Itself it guides the poet and rules his muse. Nabokov's art, on the other hand, lies beyond his fate, remaining firmly within the writer's hands. A chance event, so welcomed by Pushkin as an outside invigorating force, becomes instead Nabokov's submissive hero, a hero he himself creates; his fate he makes into a heroine. And both invariably are under their author's supervision: "My characters are galley slaves" (*SO*, I#7, 95). As Clarence Brown, a scholar of Russian literature, pointed out, fate is Nabokov's own muse (ibid.).

Don't obey thy God, O Muse! Don't ever!—insists Nabokov with all his creative might.

According to this kind of artistic construction, an odd chance insubordinate to man's will should be pitilessly driven out. This world, where life, the future, and events are canceled by the wish of a petty tyrant or a stern god, should be brought into proper order. The way to do it is to become one's own deity, a Creator, responsible for one's own fate and the fates of one's characters. In rewriting his life, in giving its current pattern the legality and stability of its rightful design, in bringing into narrative order otherwise senseless and scattered odd events, Nabokov had only himself to rely on. The tragic (or even happy) vicissitudes of life in his universe became just fragments of a bigger ornament, small pieces of the clever English puzzles that absorbed him as a child: "the thousand bits of a jigsaw puzzle gradually formed an English hunting scene; what had seemed to be the limb of a horse would turn out to belong to an elm and the hitherto unplaceable piece would snugly fill up a gap in the mottled background, affording

one the delicate thrill of an abstract and yet tactile satisfaction"
(*SM*, 27).

Those separate pieces had no force outside of the pattern the
author imposed on his life: "Coincidence of pattern is one of the
wonders of nature" (*SM*, 120).

But no matter how much Nabokov insisted on his freedom
from gods, he still sought self-assurance in a grand cosmic design.
A born aristocrat, Nabokov held that the universe originally had a
proper hierarchic order wherein the writer indeed was entitled to
an elite, special place, before chance and capricious fate interfered:

> If he had not been certain (as he also was in the case of
> literary creation) that the realization of the scheme al-
> ready existed in some other world, from which he trans-
> ferred it into this one, then the complex and prolonged
> work on the board would have been an intolerable burden
> to the mind, since it would have to concede, together with
> the possibility of realization, the possibility of its impossi-
> bility. (*G*, 171)

Elsewhere in *The Gift* he (and his character) reflect:

> It is a funny thing, when you imagine yourself returning
> into the past with the contraband of the present, how
> weird it would be to encounter there, in unexpected
> places, the prototypes of today's acquaintances, so young
> and fresh, who in a kind of lucid lunacy do not recognize

you; thus a woman, for instance, whom one loves since yesterday, appears as a young girl, standing practically next to one in a crowded train, while the chance passerby who fifteen years ago asked you the way in the street now works in the same office as you. Among this throng of the past only a dozen or so faces would acquire this anachronistic importance: low cards transfigured by the radiance of the trump. And then how confidently one could . . . (*G*, 41–42)

In some other time and space, eternal and superhuman, paper has been lined for man—now a god for himself—to rescore his life, to set to music his own, more beautiful, worthy, and harmonious composition: "A sense of security, of well-being, of summer warmth pervades my memory. That robust reality makes a ghost of the present. . . . Everything is as it should be, nothing will ever change, nobody will ever die" (*SM*, 56). With this elevating, optimistic resolution, Nabokov concludes a chapter of his memoirs.

In *Drugie berega* the incongruity of two realities, of the perfect imagined past and the defective existing present, is even more pronounced: "That reality is so bright that in comparison the Parker pen in my hand, and the hand itself with its aging luster on the already blotchy skin, seem to me nothing more than a tasteless lie" (*DB*, 173).

Later, Timofey Pnin can go on living only by convincing himself that untangling the pattern of a seemingly senseless life can

help him to overcome death. Feverish little Timosha "set himself
to solve a dreary riddle" (*Pnin*, 375) on the wallpaper in his room:

> He . . . was bothered by the undismissable fact that he
> could not find what system of inclusion and circumscrip-
> tion governed the horizontal recurrence of the pattern;
> that such a recurrence existed was proved by his being
> able to pick out here and there . . . the reappearance of
> this or that element of the series. . . . It stood to reason
> that if the evil designer—the destroyer of minds, the
> friend of fever—had concealed the key of the pattern
> with such monstrous care, that key must be as precious as
> life itself and, when found, would regain for Timofey
> Pnin his everyday health, his everyday world; and this
> lucid—alas, too lucid—thought forced him to persevere
> in the struggle. (ibid.)

Reconstructing a missing pattern soothes a loss. It restores the
meaning of one's former life; it renews hope that there will be new
prospects for new patterns: an untarnished, better world can be
assembled from once broken, scattered pieces. This recreation of
a pattern is indeed "the true purpose of autobiography" (*SM*, 16).

"The man is the book," writes Sebastian Knight in his other
book *The Doubtful Asphodel*, "unquestionably his masterpiece"
(*RLSK*, 172–73). Books are marks we leave in a world that goes
on without us. They are manifestations of our lives. Through
them we overcome death. They give us an illusion of immortality;

they allow us to achieve parity with the gods; they win back the past and conquer the future. Isn't this really the reason why many of Nabokov's characters—Humbert in *Lolita,* Felix in *Despair,* Sebastian Knight in *The Real Life of Sebastian Knight,* Kinbote in *Pale Fire,* and others—are writers themselves? They are trying to immortalize their life before, having run its course, it disappears into oblivion.

But these are his characters, the lesser writers under Nabokov's masterful supervision, while he himself, the highest authorial deity, could not trust in simple marks and manifestations—in merely creating works of art, as did amiable Pushkin, for example, or his frivolous hero Mozart[12]—they threw around their divine masterpieces like some scanty pocket change. In an unpredictable universe full of revolutions, dangers, and destruction even books didn't promise an absolute guarantee for eternity, order, and justice. In the post-1917-Revolution world, émigré artists turned out to be too fragile, too poetic, too unearthly, too wasteful in their imagery and their talent. After all, in a non-Russian, modern, "disenchanted," dispassionate, wide world, God only helps those who help themselves. Meanwhile Russian-speaking Ivan Bunin and Vladislav Khodasevich will always remain émigré poets, torn from their native Russian literature, but unable to enter the broader world canons.

Trusting neither God, nor past, nor future (at times perhaps doubting his own literary gift), Nabokov takes on even the vicissitudes of capricious fate, trying to prevent them from affecting his readers' reaction. As invulnerable as he might have seemed, as a human being (despite everything he was still a human being) he couldn't help but doubt (at least once in a while) the success of his quest to win over time, to overcome the borders of geography, of mortality. It would be foolish indeed to trust that years later we, his budding Russian audience, should read him exactly the way he himself wished to be read—who knows how the fickle populace will change over the centuries? Therefore, he couldn't leave his legacy to chance. From his position in the past, he had to ensure that a future public would follow his rules for interpretation.

And . . . here is a brilliant solution! Nabokov puts on his own miraculous show, mesmerizing his readers with astonishing manipulations, with speedy and precise strokes of his pen, exciting them by his phrases, his words, and his heroes. He seems to be saying: Look how well I do it. Past, future—all the props fit perfectly together on my enchanting stage with its black velvet backdrop; see how expertly I've managed it all. . . . But don't trespass, don't come too near, watch from afar, otherwise the magic will disappear, the show will collapse . . .

Someone once remarked to Nabokov, "In your books it seems to me that you seem to take an almost perverse delight in literary deception." He responded, "The fake move in a chess problem, the illusion of a solution or the conjuror's magic: I used to be a little conjuror when I was a boy" (*SO*, I#2, 11).

Nabokov, the prose writer, is a great conjuror, although he may not be a true wizard. His magic is stage magic: consider

Khodasevich's observation that "Sirin doesn't mask his devices at all, . . . on the contrary: Sirin displays them himself, immediately showing the laboratory of his magic."[13] The top hat with the rabbit inside, the coloring powders—it's all sleight of hand, a simulation of true sorcery. The optimistic formula, "nothing will ever change, nobody will ever die," is a hypnotist's device, not the passionate mantra of a "gaudily painted savage"—a believer in ghosts. Poetic Pushkin, on the other hand, is a true sorcerer: his Naina in the fairytale *Ruslan and Lyudmila* (1820) or the Mozart of *Mozart and Salieri*—those who trust in fate may not be spared death but they remain forever free from the fear of being unborn, unmemorable, unmentioned.

"Work is palpable in Sirin's book," Khodasevich writes in a review of *The Defense*, "In it there is that noble artificiality which inevitably and necessarily accompanies all art. . . . Sirin's novel is 'crafted,' but such 'craft' is not accessible to everyone."[14] Khodasevich carefully crafts his own words as if apologizing for Nabokov's laboriousness and calculation: indeed, praises of craftsmanship and artificiality rather than artistic inspiration could hardly convince the Russian audience, raised on miracles and metaphors. And note, in a later letter to another twentieth-century émigré writer, Nina Berberova, Khodasevich himself admits, "All of a sudden I got tired of Sirin . . . next to you he is somewhat artificial [poddelnyi]."[15]

Really, just compare all Nabokov stands for with a darling and delight of the Russians, the famous story "Levsha" ("The

Left-handed Man"), written by the nineteenth-century author Nikolai Leskov. Its hero, Levsha, the left-handed blacksmith, is capable of intuitively doing ingenious work that none of his Western (English, mind you) right-handed counterparts can do, despite their technical equipment, modern appliances, and scientific knowledge. With his able left hand he shoes a flea, while those foreigners cannot even see the flea without a microscope, let alone detect the flea's legs. Obviously, from a rational standpoint this endeavor begs a question—why shoe a flea at all? However, Russia has proudly considered itself a "left-handed"— artistic and inspired—civilization.[16]

Yet when we read Nabokov today, half a century later, when the Russian communal brotherhood or Soviet socialist unity have weakened to some extent, it would be unfair to deny him greatness because he, mistrusting providential favors or divine magic, took personal responsibility for his miracles and mirages. Contemporary pragmatism and competitiveness should see it as folly to trust anyone but oneself.

With today's open borders it is the conjuror, not the sorcerer, who would save us from God's injustice or fate's mistakes. If miracles do not respond to man's will (the world now is too big, too diverse—God cannot follow everything, cannot help everyone), a trick can always be tailored to fit mortal hopes. An experienced conjuror can enliven the dream of something improbable, and for a moment—however short—may restore, if not universal justice, at least an illusion of it.

A trick with matches, which General Kuropatkin showed five-year-old Volodya, became magic not fifteen years later when the general, disguised as a peasant, asked Nabokov's father for a cigarette, but when the author of *Speak, Memory* almost five decades later defined this "match theme" (*SM*, 15–16), that is, "the following of such thematic designs through one's life" (ibid.), as the meaning of one's fate—the true purpose of a life story.

In Nabokov's world, mirage, miracle, truth, reality, and deception are all phenomena of the same order. The conjuror's art is not easy, and life is hard, but in it, as in a masterful performance, everything adds up: a magic hat with a rabbit and coloring powders, lit matches, and chance meetings are interwoven into one exciting and exquisite, if occasionally sad, tapestry.

"Every creator is a plotter; and all the pieces impersonating his ideas on the board were here as conspirators and sorcerers. Only in the final instant was their secret spectacularly exposed" (*G*, 172),—states the narrator in *The Gift*, linking effort, magic, art, and illusion.

Some critics may argue that all art is a deception, a mirage, a fiction, which either grows out of life or into it. Even Nabokov, who routinely refused reality—"reality is a very subjective affair. I can only define it as a kind of gradual accumulation of information; and as specialization" (*SO*, I#2, 10)—once admitted that "what we call art is nothing more than just the fictional truth of life" (PPP, 550). But his own exclusive gift was that his art never even bothered to imitate surrounding reality. On the contrary, the word "reality" perplexed him: "To be sure there is an average reality, perceived by all of us, but that is not true reality: it is only the reality of general ideas, conventional forms of humdrummery, current editorials. . . . Paradoxically, the only real, authentic worlds are, of course, those that seem unusual" (*SO*, I#9, 118).

Nabokov is a mirage of a mirage, a reflection of a reflection—he re-creates and gives significance to a departed, vanished life; he makes posthumous sense of geographies and heroes, when not only the places or the people, but their meanings are long gone: "The sense of leaving Russia was totally eclipsed by the agonizing thought that Reds or no Reds, letters from Tamara would be still coming, miraculously and needlessly, to southern Crimea, and would search there for a fugitive addressee, and weakly flap about like bewildered butterflies set loose in an alien zone, at the wrong altitude, among unfamiliar flora" (*SM*, 196).

Overcoming time, space, and expatriation with the skill of a virtuoso illusionist, Nabokov performs "a feat of lucky endurance, of paradoxically detached will power" (*SO*, I#16, 177).

An unbending engineer of his fate and his heroes, he possessed a remarkable talent for concentrating his suffering in verbal constructions, making reason, not emotion, its master. Unlike his Russian predecessors he didn't create his masterpieces in order to define life (Fyodor Dostoevsky) or escape it (Nikolai Gogol), he crafted them to conquer it.

Here is a passage from Nabokov's personal diary, originally not intended for publication, in which the writer describes the evening his father was shot in Berlin: it was "something *outside life,* monstrously slow, like those mathematical puzzles that torment us in feverish half-sleep."[17] Even at the recollection of this most painful moment, Nabokov keeps his grief, no doubt unbearable, in artistic check, making of it a disciplined figure of speech.

Forbidding himself misery, he won't indulge others in their so Russian-felt weaknesses, refusing sympathy to less willful, although perhaps more worthy, persons. As a Russian saying goes, "A strong man can't comprehend the weak." And so the prose writer, who thought of himself as "good-natured," has kind words for no one. Even old Ivan Bunin is no more than an occasion for Nabokov to sharpen his wit:

I had always preferred his little-known verse to his celebrated prose. [Is that really a surprise?—N. K.] . . . At the time I found him tremendously perturbed by the personal problem of aging. The first thing he said to me was to remark with satisfaction that his posture was better than mine, despite his being some thirty years older than I. He was basking in the Nobel prize he had just received and invited me to some kind of expensive and fashionable eating place in Paris for a heart-to-heart talk. Unfortunately I happen to have a morbid dislike for restaurants and cafés, especially Parisian ones—I detest crowds, harried waiters, Bohemians, vermouth concoctions, coffee, *zakuski,* floor shows, and so forth. . . . Heart-to-heart talks, confessions in the Dostoevskian manner, are also not in my line. Bunin, a spry old gentleman, with a rich and unchaste vocabulary, was puzzled by my irresponsiveness to the hazel grouse of which I had had enough in my childhood and exasperated by my refusal to discuss eschatological matters. Toward the end of the meal we were utterly bored with each other. . . . I wanted to help Bunin into his raglan but he stopped me with a proud gesture of his open hand. Still struggling perfunctorily—*he* was now trying to help *me*—we emerged into the pallid bleakness of a Paris winter day. My companion was about to button his collar when a look of surprise and distress twisted his handsome features. Gingerly opening his overcoat, he began tugging at something under his armpit. I came to his assistance and together we finally dragged out of his sleeve my long woolen scarf which the girl stuffed into the wrong coat. The thing came out inch by inch; it was like unwrapping a mummy and we kept slowly revolving around each other in the process. . . . Then, when the operation was over, we walked on without a word to a street corner where we shook hands and separated. (*SM*, 223–24)

A brilliant literary scene! A heartless human one!

Solus Rex, deriding everyone, regardless of their position, mind, reputation, or talent, mocks us all; all who can't immediately turn the bleakness of everyday reality into a magical deception, all who suffer and who naturally fear the flow of time, the hardships, the old age . . .

Edmund Wilson, at first Nabokov's closest literary ally and then his no less formidable nemesis, accused his rival of meanness, of trampling others because he himself had a hard time handling emigration.[18] Nabokov in turn accused Wilson of failure (and fear) to assess great reputations solely according to the quality of their possessors' works: "Mr. Wilson is horrified by my 'instinct to take digs at great reputations.' . . . I refuse to be guided and controlled by a communion of established views and academic traditions" (*SO*, A#4, 266).

I won't hold against Nabokov his disagreements with conventional wisdom on what constitutes a great writer. In fact, I would agree with him that we shouldn't think that someone is great because the *New York Times* has told us to think so. Public opinion, according to Alexis de Tocqueville, can create its own brand of tyranny: "If democratic peoples substituted the absolute power of a majority for all the various powers that used excessively to impede or hold back the upsurge of individual thought, the evil itself would only have changed its form."[19] In a totalitarian society, everyone starts thinking as one man because they are obliged to; in a democratic one, everyone does so because of the unquestioning faith in public opinion. So, the more a man thinks for himself the better: "Isolation means liberty and discovery" (*SO*, I#12, 139).

However, I wouldn't completely discount Mr. Wilson's claim. Nabokov's sneering at other writers *could* indeed be explained by his own hurt and hardship. Somewhat an emigrant myself (although in a post-USSR nonpolitical, choice-based expatriate version), I truly sympathize with his predicament—challenges that always, even in the best of circumstances, face a foreigner *na drugikh beregakh* should inevitably make him tougher, no-nonsense, even curt.

Still, you may not care for some works by Conrad, Hemingway, Dostoevsky, Bunin, or Maugham, but that doesn't mean you have to cut them down at every opportunity. When asked whom he considers notable in modern literature, Nabokov almost invariably answers, "I'd much prefer to speak of the modern books that I hate at first sight" (*SO*, I#9, 116). He does suggest that, indeed, "There are several such writers [that I follow with great pleasure], but I shall not name them. Anonymous pleasure hurts nobody" (ibid., I#7, 102).[20] Well . . . it can't make anyone happy either.

In constructing a world where only he, V. N. (or "Visible Nature" [*SO*, I#14, 153], to which he once compared himself), should rule and prosper, Nabokov attempted to scale the heights of Olympus not only on the strength of natural talent and superhuman will, but also by shutting out or shutting down everyone around him—friends, enemies, any possible competition, weak or strong . . .

Michael Wood once commented with disappointment, "Nabokov was not big enough to allow himself to have great enemies. He portrayed everybody around him as unworthy, in order to look better in his own eyes, in the eyes of the world. Perhaps that's why he so tightly controls all possible responses to himself and his books. He spent his whole life not only writing his books, but also depicting himself the way he thought he should be read and understood. And this is petty and greedy—unworthy of a genius."[21]

Abram Tertz memorably explained the virtues of being happy-go-lucky in his book on Pushkin: "The lazy genius of Pushkin-Mozart is incapable of villainy, because villainy . . . originates in vain attempts to correct fate arbitrarily, to impose the principle of envy on fate through blood and deception."[22]

According to this scheme, Nabokov is not Mozart but Salieri (without the bloody overtones, of course). Nabokov, like Salieri, husbands his talent; he calculates his possibilities and considers his options. A "covetous knight"[23] of artistic creation, he doesn't waste his gifts on trifles such as the frivolous rhymes of *Dolya-Volya* or *Liubov-Krov* (Love-Blood, another favorite of Pushkin). Dissatisfied with his God-given lot in life, he takes control of his odds—and his words.

But shouldn't a genius, a real genius, be generous? He ought not to worry about such little things as his place in history or in the literary canon. Nabokov insisted, naturally, that he took a longer view: "I am immune to the convulsions of fame" (*SO*, I#11, 133). But his attacks on all comers suggest otherwise: he's indifferent to fame only as long as he's the one picking the winners.

There is a famous anecdote about Pushkin and Adam Mickiewicz, the celebrated nineteenth century Polish poet. They met
and were equally impressed with each other.

MICKIEWICZ: I've finally met Pushkin. He is almost as great a
genius as I am.

PUSHKIN: I was introduced to Mickiewicz today. What a genius![24]

OSIP MANDELSHTAM AS CINCINNATUS C.

As a prose writer Vladimir Nabokov was always kinder to poets
than to novelists. "My personal impression is that despite political
hardships, the best poetry was written in Europe in the last
twenty years (and the worst prose) was written in the Russian language,"[25] he wrote in 1941. Although he did praise Mikhail
Zoshchenko, Ilya Ilf, Yevgeny Petrov, and Yuri Olesha[26] for their
talent as prose writers, albeit comic ones (*SO*, I#6, 87), most of their
humor—kind, warm, and emotionally Russian, not derogatory but
compassionate—did not pose any competitive danger to the sarcastic, word-playing and pun-constructing witty talent of Vladimir
Nabokov.

Besides, it was still the time when Russian prose didn't (and
couldn't due to the sealed borders of the communist motherland)
reflect the possibility of living and succeeding in a borderless and
assertive open world. Russia was still too impractical, too poetic,
as were the skills of the noble Russian *intelligent,* so familiar to us
from Chekhov's *Three Sisters, Ivanov,* or *Uncle Vanya.*[27] While this

prose made it easier to tolerate suffering under the cruel Soviet regime, it didn't make it easier to live. Bulgakov, Zoshchenko, Olesha, and their characters were surviving the brutality of their time by creating a hypothetical reality of humor, fiction, and soul. Even decades later, after Ivanov and the three sisters had become part of history as characters of prerevolutionary classics, in the 1940s Russian prose was still stuck on its Chekhovian plane— only now the enclosed universe of the Russian country estate was replaced by an even more enclosed socialist country. As Nabokov's Soviet contemporaries approached the mid-twentieth-century mark they may have no longer wanted to stay in the cherry orchard (by then turned into the gulag by the brutal Stalin regime), but had no idea how to get out of it. It could well be precisely for that reason that Nabokov called Russian prose "the worst": it didn't meet the expectations and requirements of an open space, already so well known to him in exile—of the geography of the world that spread beyond the imprisoning web of Russia's enormous yet isolated steppes and communal forests.

No wonder Nabokov's main aspiration was to be the world's best prose stylist, not the world's most famous poet (could there really be one?). His quest was to teach agonizing, metaphorical and poetic Russians to live "normalno" (normally).[28] For a Russian poetic soul, the rational United States, for example, seems to respect poetry but isn't overwhelmingly interested in it. There are of course many fine American poets; they, however, do not penetrate the public consciousness as they do in Russia: few people would go around quoting by heart the whole oeuvre of Allen Ginsberg, Sylvia Plath, or Robert Frost, as the Russians do with Alexander Pushkin or Anna Akhmatova. Poetry as art is too emotional, often untranslatable, full of images and similes that meddle unnecessarily with the local utilitarian sense of everyday pragmatism.

Therefore, Nabokov's prose, even long before his American years, negated all this tortuous soul-searching, and despite its Russian linguistic representation was already American in style. In trying to express itself in strict forms, it then aspired to reflect and replicate those forms in all the shining mirrors of the world.

From a handful of poets Vladimir Nabokov admired (and apart from a few he translated) only Alexander Pushkin, Vladislav Khodasevich, and Osip Mandelshtam[29] each received individual attention in his writing. The most important, of course, is the translation-commentary on Pushkin's *Eugene Onegin*. In 1939 he dedicated his praise to Khodasevich in "On Hodasevich" (*SO*, A#1, 223–27), although Nabokov would not be Nabokov if he hadn't immediately diminished his own admiration: "I remember Vladislav Hodasevich, the greatest poet of his time, removing his dentures to eat in comfort, just as a grandee would do in the past" (ibid., I#6, 89), as if a comparison with this "grandee" should cancel out an unappealing personal commentary.

Osip Mandelshtam got his own acclaim in "On Adaptation" (1969), a critique of Robert Lowell's translation of Mandelshtam's "Za gremuchuyu doblest gryaduschikh vekov"—"For the sake of the resonant valor of ages to come" (*SO*, A#6, 280).

Furthermore, Mandelshtam, surprisingly, never suffered from Nabokov's sharp pen.

In his article on Mandelshtam, Nabokov goes into particular details of why a good translation should be faithful to the imagery of the original with the "rigor of fierce fidelity" (*SO*, A#6, 282). Rhetorically "On Adaptation" resembles the *Eugene Onegin* commentary—"In translating its 5500 lines into English I had to decide between rhyme or reason—and I chose reason" (ibid., I#1, 7): "In transposing *Eugene Onegin* from Pushkin's Russian into my English I have sacrificed to completeness of meaning every formal element save the iambic rhythm: its retention assisted rather than hindered fidelity. . . . To my ideal literalism [certain types of literalism may be necessary in English after all—N. K.] I sacrificed everything . . . that the dainty mimic prizes higher than truth" (*EO*, 1:x).

Similarly, Nabokov agrees that Lowell's may be a good English poem, but the adaptation of an original masterpiece is "something very like cruelty and deception" (*SO*, A#6, 283). Elsewhere he uses analogous language to describe Mandelshtam's political fate as well.

In fact, uncharacteristically, Nabokov glorified Mandelshtam even more because of his political fate: "In my boyhood . . . I also knew him by heart, but he gave me a less fervent pleasure [than Alexander Blok]. Today, through the prism of a tragic fate, his poetry seems greater than it actually is" (*SO*, I#7, 97). As a rule Nabokov never considered a sad political fate a cause for praise.

Rather he took great pride in being antipolitical and antihistorical: "Nothing bores me more than political novels and the literature of social intent" (*SO*, I#1, 3); "My second favorite fact about myself is . . . that since my youth . . . my political creed has remained as bleak and changeless as an old gray rock" (ibid., I#3, 34).

Appraising Boris Pasternak,[30] for example, Nabokov conceded that although he "deeply sympathized with [his] predicament in a police state; yet neither the vulgarities of the *Zhivago* style nor a philosophy that sought refuge in a sickly sweet brand of Christianism could ever transform that sympathy into a fellow writer's enthusiasm" (*SO*, I#22, 206). Some of us may agree with this literary assessment of *Doctor Zhivago*—elsewhere Nabokov cleverly changes Zhivago's name into Mertvago (*Ada*, 409)[31]—but the fact of the matter is that the complicated political fate of Boris Pasternak never influenced Nabokov's attitude towards his writing.

After reading *On Socialist Realism* by the dissident Abram Tertz, Vladimir Vladimirovich responded even to him, a labor camp prisoner, with competitiveness rather than compassion. According to Brian Boyd's biography, he commented that although Tertz's case was stated with intelligence and brilliancy, he, Nabokov, had been saying the same to his students for twenty years,[32] as if the safe campuses of Wellesley, Harvard, and Cornell could be at all comparable to the Socialist Realist camps of Dubrovlag.

So there is no politics, no sympathy for political martyrs . . . unless they are Nabokov's own characters. Throughout Nabokov's novels we encounter Osip Mandelshtam's fate, both poetic and political—in *Invitation to a Beheading*, but also in *Tyrants Destroyed*, and even *Bend Sinister*.

Such an intertextual weaving of the poet's life into the writer's work requires a brief commentary on a certain affinity between Nabokov and Mandelshtam as artists and men.

Their most apparent similarity is the gravitation towards rationalized individual Westernness versus communal Russianness. Nabokov is a Russian writer who, due to his geographical exile, aspired to and succeeded in becoming a Western one. Mandelshtam, originally Jewish, passed over physically uncomfortable Russianism in favor of spiritual exile into Westernism in the form of Protestant and then Catholic Christianity.

In his notes on Pyotr Chaadaev, Mandelshtam asserts that "The West, when discovered by a Russian, becomes more concentrated, more concrete than the historical West itself."[33] And then he adds, "How many of us spiritually emigrated to the West [in search of individual freedom]. . . . How many live subconsciously divided, their bodies here, while their souls remain there!"

For Nabokov the emigrant, his own physical living in the West "confirms [him] in [his] favorite habit, the habit of freedom" (*SO*, I#13, 149). He shared with Mandelshtam Chaadaev's quest for individual freedom, but Nabokov indeed was "lucky" to have his free "body there" while Mandelshtam had to create freedom inside himself, relying solely on the strength of his spirit. Already in 1908, long before his Soviet suffering began, Mandelshtam wrote, "But I love my miserable country, / having known no other."[34]

In *Speak, Memory* the exiled Nabokov makes a sad statement: "One is always at home in one's past" (*SM*, 87). For Mandelshtam even this was a luxury. The cruelty of socialist surroundings forced the poet to look beyond his personal past and personal home and to find affinity with infinity—with the *mirozdanie* (universe).

If Nabokov, according to Edmund Wilson, was unhappy and therefore awarded unhappiness to others,[35] Mandelshtam was generous to humanity because of his own sorrows. At least in poetry he spares it a horrible, tragic fate, ending all misfortunes with a fairytale conclusion:

> *It's cold in Europe. In Italy it's dark.*
> *Power is disgusting, like a barber's hands.*
> *And yet he calls himself noble, more slyly than ever,*
> *And smiles, through the open window . . .*
> *Maybe, gentle Ariosto, a century will pass,*
> *And we'll pour your blue-sky and our Black-Sea*
> *In a single broad brotherly blueness.*
> *We've been there, too.*[36]

Furthermore, he suggests that even if Western, "civilized" Europe had to go through some cruel times in the past—"We've been there, too"—then Russia's totalitarian case may not remain its destiny forever.

In "Poet o sebe" ("A Poet on Himself") Mandelshtam writes: "The October Revolution could not have not influenced my work, as it deprived me of my 'biography,' the feeling, the understanding of my own personal importance. And I am grateful because it has ended once and for all my sense of spiritual well-being and my living off the cultural capital of the past."[37]

In "Shum Vremeni" ("The Noise of Time") he confesses:

> My desire is to speak not about myself but to track down the age, the noise, and the germination of time. My memory is inimical to all that is personal. If it depended on me, I should only make a wry face in remembering the past. I was never able to understand the Tolstoys and the Aksakovs, all those grandsons Bagrov, enamored of family archives with their epic domestic memoirs. My memory is not loving but inimical, and it labors not to reproduce but to distance the past.[38]

After the Bolshevik Revolution Nabokov had also to reinvent himself on other shores. He also had to give up his own "cultural [that is, aristocratic] capital," but he, on the other hand, is by no accounts "grateful." *Speak, Memory* lovingly "labors to reproduce, not to distance" his personal past: an account of the Nabokovs' political, cultural, and aristocratic importance, their distinguished family tree, their Batovo estate where Pushkin may have dueled with Ryleev[39] (*SM*, 44). And then we read a passage from one of the interviews: "Our house was one of the first where young Shalyapin sang, and I have fox-trotted with Pavlova in London half a century ago" (*SO*, I#15, 171).

Though Mandelshtam had no aristocratic background, his troubles were no less tragic. Unlike Nabokov's, his suffering was not nostalgic, projected onto the past—"In a way Nabokov went through all the sorrows and delights of nostalgia long before the Revolution had removed the scenery of his young years" (OCE, 249)—but it was a very concrete physical menace to his life. The looming threat of death made him much freer not to be obsessed with his own history. Misery, which he had aspired to survive, allowed him to be more generous to men, history and time:

> *With all the squeaking, creaking world-boots*
> *What a lightweight bed.*
> *All right, so what: if we can't design*
> *A new time, let's spend a hundred years here.*[40]

Even to the torturous Soviet regime his sympathy is overwhelmingly Christ-like: "A terrified bureaucrat—face like a mattress— / No one on earth more pitiful, absurd."[41]

Designing his life's retrospective, Nabokov explained that "the following of . . . thematic designs through one's life should be, I think, the true purpose of autobiography" (*SM*, 16). Each one's life (and certainly, Nabokov's—*Solus Rex*) is justified because it has a definite, unique, individual pattern in an infinite, eternal universe, while the universe itself serves only as a background, a canvas for each single, personal story.

Mandelshtam, on the other hand, has to trust not his own, but universal history to be ultimately just—dying may be acceptable only if his personal unfortunate living was part of a larger eternal historical justice, in which a single man's misfortunes do not guarantee worldwide misery: "Not many live for eternity— / But think about here, about now, / And it turns frightening, the walls won't hold!"[42] he writes already in 1912, when still very young.

Nabokov *wants* the reader to think he is marvelous. He knows how to make us believe in his greatness. A magnificent conjuror, a brilliant illusionist, he masterfully lures us in, enchants us, puts us in his debt. But since Nabokov distrusts *obshchei* (general, universal) history, which once upset the destined order by taking away the grandeur of his noble heritage, he chooses to depend only on his own talent to reconstruct a personally meaningful version of the pre-1917 past in order to continue living. By doing so, he lacks the comfort of Mandelshtam's more than personal relations to not only *his* but *our* world, *our* eternity, with its infinity, with everything having a harmonious place in it, despite the cruelty of the moment. Mandelshtam *is* marvelous because of his genuine carefree Pushkinian nature—"his sense of life as something endowed with meaning . . . his view of the world as a settled abode."[43]

For both Nabokov and Mandelshtam, the "habit of freedom," whatever form it takes, spiritual or physical, requires solitude and individuality—a necessity to think for oneself with aversion to groups and to the communal style of the Russian *sobornoe* (united, collective) mentality, which brought the accursed, sweeping revolution in the first place.

Both Mandelshtam and Nabokov are not *kak vse* (like everyone else), separate from the communal crowd. (On the other hand, is there an artist who is not different from the mass? There is a famous photograph of Joseph Brodsky: a crowd, people with their heads turned back walking away from us, the viewers, and Brodsky, his back to this crowd, facing us, trying to break through.) Nabokov states, "communal aura involuntarily prejudices me against a novel" (*SO*, I#8, 113), while Mandelshtam affirms that "the true writer [is] the mortal enemy of literature," which "always and everywhere carries out one assignment: it helps superiors keep their soldiers obedient and it helps judges execute reprisals against doomed men."[44]

Each, however, emphasizes different aspects of this individuality.

Nabokov is different from the world (and the literary world) for himself—"Isolation means liberty and discovery"; "Philosophically, I am an indivisible monist" (*SO*, I#6, 85).

Mandelshtam is different from the world for the world—even before the Revolution, in 1914, he had already come to an understanding that "There is a freedom / inhabited by spirit—the fate of the best."[45] He then continued in the 1930s during the height of Stalin's repressions, "And I read your primer, alone, Infinity, all alone." "No comparisons: everyone alive is incomparable," he warned, predicting then in the "Poem on an Unknown Soldier": "I'll be the light of the world."[46]

Mandelshtam's solitary inimitability is not a geographical exile, the external exile we usually associate with émigré anguish, but an inner exile—a heroic exile in the spirit, similar not to Nabokov's, but to that of his tormented characters, Cincinnatus C. or Adam Krug.

I am not suggesting, of course, that there should be any distinction between "heroic" and "nonheroic" exile, just as there could be no calculation of different degrees of suffering—all unhappy families are unhappy in their own way—but still, Mandelshtam's inner emigration is, at least in Russia, by far the greatest example of a spiritual expatriation into a firm bastion of one's own creativity.

Mandelshtam always admired in Chaadaev his desire "to run away, as if from the plague, from this shapeless paradise"—Russia with its "great Slavic dream . . . of total spiritual disarmament, after which there should come some uncertain state, called *mir* [peace, world]."[47]

His entire life was an emigration of the spirit into a historical eternity from the "shapeless paradise" of the Russian communal *mir,* which often took the form of a police state precisely because of this shapelessness. "We cling to form because we have not enough of it; probably it is the only thing we have not enough of; we have never had and never can have either hierarchy or structure (we are too spiritual for this), and move freely from nihilism to conservatism and back again,"[48] said Abram Tertz to explain the usual Russian transformation from the idea of total love to the idea of total control over this love.

For lack of a better option Mandelshtam preferred to live not in this shapeless, formless Russian land but in history as in space, in the universe as in time. This kind of initiation into some historical realm beyond reality required an exceptional and rare bravery—*muzhestvennost*. In "O prirode slova" ("On the Nature of the Word") Mandelshtam asserts, "A man should be brave."[49] Nabokov agrees that "the best quality [of a man] is to be fearless" (*SO*, I#13, 152). They both were, both had to be courageous, but if viewed through the lenses of the Russian tradition of heroic suffering, Vladimir Nabokov's fearlessness is inferior to the bravery of Osip Mandelshtam.

Mandelshtam's political fate matched his poetic one. A man and a poet, weak and tormented, he was nonetheless kind and courageous. Nabokov instead awarded exploits to his heroic heroes, while himself admitting, "As a human specimen I present no particular fascination" (*SO*, I#14, 157).

Hence, he re-created (even if unintentionally) the heroic fate of Osip Mandelshtam in the tale of Cincinnatus C., "a poet" from Nabokov's "dreamiest and most poetical novel" *Invitation to a Beheading* (*SO*, I#6, 76). Cincinnatus, whose only sin is his opaque nature in a transparent world (a reference to Zamyatin's *We*, despite Nabokov's "loathing [of] science fiction" [ibid., I#9, 117]?), is a solitary, fragile, ineloquent prisoner with no trust in words.

"Oh, no, I do not gloat over my own person; . . . I have no desires, save the desire to express myself—in defiance of all the world's muteness. How frightened I am. How sick with fright. But no one shall take me away from myself" (*ITB*, 91), pleads Cincinnatus when invited to a beheading.

In this sentiment we recognize Mandelshtam's paralyzing feeling of fear: "Animal fear taps on the typewriters, animal fear proofreads the gibberish on sheets of toilet paper, scribbles denunciations, hits men when they're down, demands execution for prisoners."[50]

The epigraph to *Invitation to a Beheading* is from *Discours sur les ombres* (*Dissertation on Shadows*) by the French philosopher Delalande (a contemporary and compatriot of the American poet John Shade):[51] "Comme un fou se croit Dieu, nous nous croyons mortels," which also evokes the fear of shadows throughout Mandelshtam's work: "Whoever's frightened by barking, and by his shadow, who's mowed by the wind—he's really unlucky, whoever's half-alive and begging alms from shadows—he's really poor."[52]

The suspicion, even hatred, that Mandelshtam has for eloquent literature—"I divide all works of world literature into those written with and without permission. The first are trash, the second—stolen air. As for writers who write things with prior permission, I want to spit in their faces,"[53]—is upheld by Cincinnatus, who is also simultaneously a poet and an enemy of literature. On the one hand, he dreams of being an artist like Pushkin: "I want to think about something else, clarify other things . . . but

I write obscurely and limply, like Pushkin's lyrical duelist" (*ITB*, 92); " 'My words all mill about in one spot,' wrote Cincinnatus. 'Envious of poets' " (ibid., 194). On the other, he recognizes that it is impossible to write "as there is in the world not a single human who can speak my language; or, more simply, not a single human who can speak; or, even more simply, not a single human" (ibid., 95). Similarly Mandelshtam feels himself as a wordless alien, lost in this world: "I am a Chinaman, no one understands me."[54]

His recurrent images of sealed, tortured, unspeaking, helpless lips and empty words could have been written by Cincinnatus. It is no coincidence that the ineloquence of Mandelshtam's family detailed in "The Noise of Time" is similar to Cincinnatus's complaints of muteness: "all my best words are deserters and do not answer the trumpet call, and the remainder are cripples" (*ITB*, 205).

Mandelshtam, the poet, agrees:

> *The pain, the pain—hunting lost words,*
> *Lifting sick eyelids,*
> *And with lime in your blood, gathering night grasses*
> *For an alien tribe.*[55]

He would rather praise a missed word: "What I prize in the doughnut is the hole. . . . Real work is Brussels lace, the main thing in it is what holds the pattern up: air, punctures, truancy."[56] When everyone is an eloquent bastard like Cincinnatus's executioner M'sieur Pierre, ineloquence becomes the sign of initiation, reason, and sense: "Jailers love to read novels and, of all men, have the greatest need of literature." Like Mandelshtam in "Chetvertaya proza" ("Fourth Prose"), hopeless Cincinnatus too would stumble in words, honoring a pause:

> Between his movement and the movement of the laggard shadow—that second, that syncope—there is a rare kind of time in which I live—the pause, the hiatus, when the heart is like a feather. . . . And I'm wrong when I keep repeating that there is no refuge in the world for me. There is! I'll find it! A lush ravine in the desert! A patch of snow in the shadow of an alpine crag! . . . What anguish, oh, what anguish. . . . And it is obvious to me that I have not yet removed the final film from my fear. (*ITB*, 53)

When asked for his last wish before his execution: " 'To finish writing something,' whispered Cincinnatus half questioningly but then he frowned, straining his thoughts, and suddenly understood that everything had in fact been written already" (*ITB*, 209). "Death" (206) was the last word he wrote and then crossed off—the *word* should become a *deed*.

According to Anna Akhmatova, after composing his most famous poem "We live, not feeling the ground under our feet,"[57] in 1933, Mandelshtam, bravely leaving his inner exile for execution, declared, "I am ready for death."[58] Another act of bravery, "The Wolf" (1931)—"For the sake of resonant valor of ages to come," which Nabokov felt so compelled to translate and defend in "On Adaptation," calling it "one of the masterpieces of Russian poetry"

(*SO*, A#6, 282), was found during a KGB search of Mandelshtam's apartment in 1934. And Mandelshtam, like Cincinnatus C.,
courageously went on to his own "beheading," to his Voronezh
exile—fragile, slender, unheroic, an incredible hero—"So steps
might sound like acts."[59]

His "Egipetskaya marka" ("Egyptian Stamp"), written in 1927,
tells the story of the always fidgeting, hapless Parnok, Mandelshtam's worse version of himself (or Cincinnatus). At the
end, however, the story makes a switch into fearless first-person
narration:

> It is terrifying to think that our life is a tale without a plot
> or hero, made up out of desolation and glass, out of fever-
> ish babble of constant digressions. . . .
>
> What a pleasure for the narrator to switch from the
> third person to the first! It is just as if, after having had to
> drink from tiny inconvenient thimble-sized glasses, one
> were suddenly to say the hell with them, to get hold of
> oneself, and drink cold, unboiled water straight out of the
> faucet.
>
> Terror takes me by the hand and leads me. . . . I love
> terror, I respect it. I almost said "With it, I'm not terri-
> fied!"[60]

And then, in a few years, in 1930, the brave "Fourth Prose"
follows. "Fourth Prose" is what Cincinnatus C. could have written, should have written, must have written, and did indeed write

as Osip Mandelshtam, one of the bravest and most tragic heroes of Vladimir Nabokov: "I have no manuscripts, no notebooks, no archives. I have no handwriting because I never write. I alone in Russia work from the voice while all around the bitch pack writes. What the hell kind of writer am I!? Get out, you fools!"[61]

In Nabokov's *Tyrants Destroyed* laughter is a "proven" tool to destroy tyrants, the only fictional tool possible. "Rereading my chronicle, I see that, in my efforts to make him terrifying, I have only made him ridiculous, thereby destroying him,"[62] the narrator satisfyingly concludes his parody of horror.

"We live, not feeling the ground under our feet" was not just fiction. This very act of laughter—"Huge cockroach whiskers laughing, / Boot-tops beaming . . . Whenever he's got a victim, he glows like a broadchested / Georgian munching a raspberry"[63]— was a very real act of bravery.

Death, which stood between fiction and reality, separates Nabokov and Mandelshtam: for Mandelshtam laughter was life (death, rather); for Nabokov it could be no more than a story, albeit a very sad one.

From an interview with Vladimir Nabokov:

The poems he [Osip Mandelshtam] heroically kept composing [in a remote concentration camp] until madness eclipsed his limpid gifts are admirable specimens of a human mind at its deepest and highest. Reading them enhances one's healthy contempt for Soviet ferocity. Tyrants

and torturers will never manage to hide their comic stum-
bles behind their cosmic acrobatics. *Contemptuous laughter
is all right, but it is not enough in the way of moral relief. And
when I read Mandelshtam's poems composed under the accursed rule of those beasts, I feel a kind of hopeless shame, being
so free to live and think and write and speak in the free part of
the world.—That's the only time when liberty is bitter.* (*SO*,
I#5, 58; my emphasis)

THE GREATER FEAT: GLORY OR KINDNESS?
(ON NABOKOV'S CHARACTERS)

How hard is it to face an execution like Cincinnatus C., to be a
weary and proud sufferer like Adam Krug, or a patient hero like
Osip Mandelshtam? It's no wonder we envy the dead the narrative logic of their lives:

Human fate is grasped ideally in the genre of tragedy,
which builds dramatically toward death. In tragedy, death
becomes the goal and stimulus for action, in the course of
which personality has time to reveal itself without with-
holding anything and, having ripened completely, fulfills
its destiny. As we watch his rapid and fatal approach to
ruin, we rejoice that the hero has been granted such
preference—that he, only just born, is equipped and in-
sured, and his entire biography arranged as preparation
for the finale. In the hero's destiny and character death is

sown like a seed, and as it sprouts before our eyes we delight in its consistency, which makes the effort of life into
a mortal feat.[64]

It is much harder to live not for this feat but for oneself when
even life itself, it seems, has turned its back on you.

Vladimir Nabokov is a post-Chekhovian step in Russian literature, a step towards its rationalization. Victor Shklovsky once
explained that "Chekhov introduce[d] the alarm clock into Russian literature."[65] Simon Karlinsky credited Chekhov with creating
"biology-oriented literary tradition" that was "uncharacteristic"
for Russian literature—a "tradition of objective and independent
literary art, not subservient to ideology, nationalism or religion."
This kind of literature refrains from didactically "offering any
solutions to problems raised, . . . settling instead for a beautifully
clear ('correct') statement to those problems."[66]

It was Chekhov who first purged Russia's Bashmachkins and
Karamazovs—conflicted, self-reflective, God-seeking, and soul-
saving heroes—of their practical quality. That is to say, Chekhov
was the first one to deromanticize their impractical qualities, their
savoring of suffering. Chekhov's heroes are magnificent: the lady
with the lapdog, the three sisters, Ivanov, Varya, Petya Trofimov,
even Ionych and Belikov.[67] But by the same token they're senseless. Proclaiming the man of flesh and blood a fiction, and the
man of myth, of soul, its great national achievement, Russian
literature broke free of earth's gravity. It created wonderful, but

emotional and failure-doomed heroes, who by the beginning of the twentieth century started losing their romantic appeal. It fell to Nabokov to bring these unearthly creatures down to earth.[68]

Nabokov, who was traditionally brought up on the high and heroic examples of Russian literature, found his own heroism in choosing an unheroic life. He made a new daring of simply keeping going in a life that was somewhat commonplace and dull. His extraordinary exploit was in the desire to endure, to find the patience and willpower for ordinariness and routine.

Nabokov was the first in Russian literature to show us that "normalcy" and *poshlost* (banality, complacency, vulgarity) aren't necessarily synonyms. Previously, whatever Charles Dickens (English literature, in which individual choices make a difference, and human behavior, good or bad, effects one's personal happiness or unhappiness) would strive for—stability and a happy ending—Nikolai Gogol (Russian literature, where life is unpredictable in imposing its own fatal logic) would flee from, breaking from everyday banality in a Troika Bird.

Nabokov unites both urges. He uncovered the secret of how to survive a life that is threatened by nothing but life itself, to survive, that is to outmaneuver, outwait, outguess, "pampering life, life—our patient" (*BS*, 13), to re-create life in one's own image and likeness.

With his patience, persistence, confidence, and talent, the American Nabokov was able to lead the Russian hero out of Chekhov's enchanted cherry orchard, untended by idealistic and impractical aristocrats and intellectuals. But it was only in *Ada,* as late as 1969, that the writer finally achieved his goal of creating fairytale-happy heroes, even though they still had to pay for their luck in love with a problematic incest.

Yet it's the very kinship of Ada and Van Veen that makes this extreme mode of "normal" happiness work. To ensure the absolute success of this "happifying" project Nabokov *had* to deprive them of natural, uncontrived (i.e. uncontrolled, spontaneous) human feelings, instead showing them matching wits, striking at one another with the cleverest puns and superhuman erudition. It's a *picture* of love, a *picture* of suffering . . .

To preserve the sublimity of this perfect artistic construction, Nabokov keeps their incestuous love apart from the mortal world. Therefore, despite the improper incest, the novel has no conflict: Van Veen ages happily, lacking a double or adversary like Hermann's Felix in *Despair* or Humbert's Quilty in *Lolita.* For the sake of the "fairytale," Ada is not Van's double but an integral part of him, his other half. She belongs to him organically, indispensably, like a hand, head, or heart, as the chapter heading "Vaniada's Adventures" (*Ada,* 409) indicates. The melancholy and boredom that periodically waft from the pages of this book are the price paid for the contentment of its heroes. Happiness after all is always somewhat boring (or as Russians put it—*poshlaya*—complacent, banal). It's no wonder that not knowing what to do with the heroes afterwards all fairytales (and Russian fairytales in particular) end with a wedding; and paradise and hell (*ad*) are equally static, equidistantly elevated to the heavens or plunged to the nether world. But then life in those tales lasts long and happily, and the end comes magically, painlessly, and simultaneously for both. In *Ada* Nabokov seems to be determined to turn the fairytale into life.

Despite the author's objection to simplified comparisons of his heroes with real people,[69] Nabokov's measured nonfictional life was remarkably similar to the fictional one of the Veens. Véra and Vladimir, "Vervolodya," also lived in their own paradise. Like Ada and Van, they were constantly sharpening their wits and competing in literary erudition.[70] And like Ada and Van, the Nabokovs did not find their controlled and calm American-Swiss heaven immediately: in 1937 Vladimir had a brief but torrid affair in Paris with the émigré Irina Yurevna Gvadanini.

But that's that, by the way. Nabokov doesn't interest us for his banal love affair. Nabokov, a "person with no public appeal" (*SO*, I#1, 3), interests us as someone who was able to create for himself fictional Van-like happiness in a nonfictional world. He interests us as the creator of Van, that "charming villain" (*ibid.*, I#13, 143), who dreams and dares to achieve the impossible, a romance with his own sister. He captivates us as the creator of other villains and heroes, in which he reflected not the husband's conflicts (a private affair) but rather the writer's conflicts between poetry and prose, art and life, heroism and ordinariness, kindness and severity, *poshlost* and "normalcy."

In inventing his daring and mad characters, Nabokov tried to keep his own "Dostoevshchina" (Dostoevsky-like horrors) in check, strictly confining it to the pages of his books: "Some of my characters are, no doubt, pretty beastly, but I really don't care, they are outside my inner self like the mournful monsters of a cathedral façade—demons placed there merely to show that they have been booted out" (*SO*, I#2, 19).

What Nabokov is saying here is that if one can't avoid writing about Raskolnikov in principle, one can at least prevent him from walking the streets with an ax. And the author of *Glory, Despair, Lolita,* and *Pale Fire* himself took pride in his private persona with no public appeal, deliberately preferring Western discipline and stability to Russian revolutions, outbursts, and daring acts. Does an artist really need to be a gambler to write about gambling? Should he proudly sleep on a bed of nails in order to be able to describe a perfect revolutionary?[71]

Moreover, should this artist, serving as a personal example to his readers, be obliged to spend his time exhuming dead bodies, placing his head on the block, going to jail, charging to the attack? In fact he should be discouraged from such mundane expressions of heroism. And if he must serve at all, then let him serve with his talent, emotions, and senses which touch our souls.

Dramatic Russian literature, however, has always been inspiring, even insisting on, the first form of "service," occasionally agreeing to settle for a second one.

I well remember how in Soviet high school we used to chide Pushkin for insufficient patriotism. He didn't march on Senate

Square in 1825[72] and thus selfishly stayed alive. (At the same time we were angry with him for later dying, equally selfishly, in a private duel.) But how great would have been the loss had Pushkin perished in the depths of Siberia two years later, leaving behind not an immortal hymn—"Vo glubine sibirskikh rud" ("In far Siberia's deepest soil")[73]—but a patriotic corpse! To the relief of readers reared in "ideological humanitarianism,"[74] Pushkin did follow (even if after the fact) in the tradition of socially conscious artistry—wrote that very poem that twentieth-century schoolchildren then memorized as an example of his revolutionary fervor:

> *Then heavy chains fall by the board,*
> *Then dungeons crack—and freedom's voices*
> *Will greet you at the gate, rejoicing,*
> *And brothers hand to you a sword.*

But even such a "service"—art for the regime or against it—was unacceptable to Nabokov: "Sometimes it may be that even the most irreproachable artist tried to say his word in defense of the dying and miserable, but one should not give in to this temptation" (PPP, 550). Really, what could be more tedious than "literature of social intent"? And if he hadn't so disapproved of sympathy for sufferers, hadn't insisted too much on his indifference to the fate of his former country, he would without doubt, fault, or sin have been excused from the Russian tradition of accomplishing feats, mortal or literary. After all, Nabokov is "an

American writer, [only] born in Russia" (*SO*, I#3, 26). Like Van Veen he lives and writes just to please himself in the happy cocoon of his Western paradise.

Once Nabokov did admit, however, that "had my Russian novels been translated [earlier into English], they might have provided a shock and a lesson for pro-Soviet enthusiasts" (*SO*, I#7, 107). Thus, whatever Nabokov might claim, his work was not entirely apolitical if he thought it could have convinced his American liberal readers of Soviet barbarity. This, in effect, was confirmed by Véra Nabokov, "Every book by VN is a blow against tyranny, every form of tyranny."[75]

Though firmly maintaining that any motive other than one's own fulfillment was irrelevant ("Why did I write any of my books, after all? For the sake of the pleasure" [*SO*, I#2, 16]), Nabokov, however, kept going back to Martin of *Glory*, his first heroic hero—and often enough to make one wonder whether the writer wasn't plagued by survivor's guilt, a common enough feeling among those who survive by chance when others die unjustly. Something, in fact, he confirmed when contemplating Osip Mandelshtam's fate: "I feel a kind of hopeless shame, being so free to live and think and write and speak in the free part of the world."

In a long interview (1966) with the literary scholar Alfred Appel, a former student, Nabokov explains Martin's exploit: *Glory* "is the story of a Russian expatriate, a romantic young man of my set and time, a lover of adventure for adventure's sake, proud flaunter of peril, climber of unnecessary mountains, who merely for the pure thrill of it decides one day to cross illegally into Soviet Russia, and then cross back to exile. Its main theme is the overcoming of fear, the glory and rapture of that victory" (*SO*, I#6, 88).

In 1938 in Paris Nabokov wrote another story, "The Visit to the Museum." Its hero winds up in contemporary Leningrad, which materializes from a hellish museum tour: "A semiphantom in a light foreign suit, I stood on the impassive snow of an October night, somewhere on the Moyka or the Fontanka Canal, or perhaps on the Obvodny, and I had to do something, go somewhere, run; desperately protect my fragile, illegal life. Oh, how many times in my sleep I had experienced a similar sensation! Now, though, it was reality" (VM, 285).

In the late forties, Nabokov gave the same account in *Speak, Memory* (at the time still *Conclusive Evidence*): "Sometimes I fancy myself revisiting [the Saint Petersburg countryside] with a false passport, under an assumed name. It could be done. But I do not think I shall ever do it. I have been dreaming of it too idly and too long" (*SM*, 195–96).

And here is the Russian version in *Drugie berega:* "I often think about going there with a fake passport under the name of Knickerbocker. I could have done that, but probably never will. I've dreamt about it for too long, too idly, and too wastefully. I have wasted a dream" (*DB*, 271).

In a poem "To Prince S. M. Kachurin" (1947), Nabokov explored the same theme, a visit to communist Saint Petersburg–Leningrad—"Kachurin, I took your advice / And for three days already I've lived / In a museum setting, in a dark blue / Parlor with a view of the Neva"[76]—plunging his readers into confusion with numerous glosses on this poetic journey.

In one of these we learn that Stefan Mstislavovich Kachurin, an old friend of Nabokov's, was a White Army colonel. "Only a heart of gold, limited mental faculties, and senile optimism could excuse him for suggesting the journey I've described," adds the author. In the notes to a different version his pal Kachurin becomes Sergei Mikhailovich, a racecar driver: "Three or four years ago the opportunity arose to visit Russia incognito, and kindly Sergei Mikhailovich ardently tried to persuade me to take advantage of it. I vividly pictured my journey there and wrote the following verses." In yet another gloss Nabokov explains that no Kachurin actually exists, but "the reader should accept [him] as my old friend—with the sort of ringing apostrophizing that Pushkin gave the names of friends in his poems."[77]

Whether Kachurin lived or not can stay Nabokov's secret, an old dissembler and deceiver. But take note that the name of the mysterious prince is mentioned in not only the Russian *Gift* but also the English *Pale Fire* and *Ada,* both written many years after *Glory.*

The Kachurin mystification only confirms the writer's conflict over senseless heroism and practical normalcy. Nabokov knew that in a Russian sense he was no hero and accused another, a friend—however real—of stupidity in order to justify himself, to sidestep his so Russian-felt shame for his failure of nerve, to us, his future Russian readers.

Nabokov did seem to have parted ways with the irrational use of emotions for needless exploits and acts: Cincinnatus C. follows Martin to the grave but now the dying hero is draped in the meditative garb of the poet—Osip Mandelshtam. And the godlike author makes it plain to Adam Krug, who's no longer even a hero but instead a genius and philosopher, that principled heroism is fatal in the struggle with totalitarianism. To show Adam the folly of taking on tyrants personally, *mano a mano,* the cruelly logical Nabokov kills off the protagonist's son, the child David. We can face tyrants with laughter—like the narrator of *Tyrants Destroyed*—or at a distance, with books—like Nabokov himself—but never should we do it—too foolish, too dramatic— in hand-to-hand combat: Adam Krug dies to prove the writer's point that "death is but a question of style, a mere literary device" (*BS*, xviii). (We can be sure that Mandelshtam, who knew torture in the very real world of the gulag, would disagree.)

Bend Sinister may be the harshest of Nabokov's works, harshest on its heroes. Sending Adam Krug to a sad death (though "rewarding" him with madness right before), the author verifies his own following assertion: the "design of my novel is fixed in my imagination and every character follows the course I imagine for him. I am the perfect dictator in that private world insofar as I alone am responsible for its stability and truth" (*SO*, I#6, 69).

In all fairness, who among us wouldn't sadly admit that the fates of both Osip Mandelshtam and Adam Krug reflect a hard

truth of life. They are only products of their time and place, narrative or geographical, and cannot help but be victims of tyrants,
real or imaginary:

> I have often noticed that we are inclined to endow our
> friends with the stability of type that literary characters
> acquire in the reader's mind. No matter how many times
> we reopen "King Lear," never shall we find the good king
> banging his tankard in high revelry, all woes forgotten, at
> a jolly reunion with all three daughters and their lapdogs.
> Never will Emma rally, revived by the sympathetic salts in
> Flaubert's father's timely tear. Whatever evolution this or
> that popular character has gone through between the
> book covers, his fate is fixed in our minds, and, similarly,
> we expect our friends to follow this or that logical and
> conventional pattern we have fixed for them. Thus X will
> never compose the immortal music that would clash with
> the second-rate symphonies he has accustomed us to.
> Y will never commit murder. . . . We have it all arranged
> in our minds, and the less often we see a particular person
> the more satisfying it is to check how obediently he con-
> forms to our notion of him every time we hear of him.
> Any deviation in the fates we have ordained would strike
> us as not only anomalous but unethical. We would prefer
> not to have known at all our neighbor, the retired hot-dog

stand operator, if it turns out he has just produced the greatest book of poetry his age has seen. (*Lolita*, 265)

Acknowledging that human fate is ideally grasped in the genre of tragedy, which builds dramatically toward death, we even more admire the noble character of a literary dictator—Nabokov the author, who tested his heroes in the mad hope of freeing them from a waking nightmare not of their making; in the vain attempt to save them from torture that real people had to endure in real Stalin's gulag. Cruelty kept in check by a narrator holds out the chance of rescue, if not now then maybe in the next book—pattern is a redemption of loss—as in novels this hope hangs magically on the author's favor, not on an arbitrary and cruel fate.

This explains Nabokov's regard for his heroes Martin, Mandelshtam, Cincinnatus, and Adam Krug. He repeats and records their exploits in hopes not only of redeeming his own lack of "physical" heroism—that alone would be too simple—but also of correcting the future, resolving their literary fate in the key of life.[78]

The writer's conflict of heroism and "normalcy" acquires still greater drama in the clash of everyday life with eternal art. Nabokov's desire to square art and life is at odds with the traditionally Russian understanding of "normalcy" as unwelcome ordinariness and *poshlost*, i.e. *poshlo* (banal) is not only what's not tragic and heroic, but also what's not even dramatic.

Therefore, Nabokov shelters the Veens from the banal happiness of their romance by a criminal act of incest because in a true Russian manner he too fears vulgarity and tedium more than anything: "What Russians call *poshlust* is beautifully timeless and so cleverly painted all over with protective tints that its presence . . . often escapes detection. . . . Literature is one of [*poshlust*'s] best breeding places. . . . *Poshlust,* it should be repeated, is especially vigorous and vicious when the sham is *not* obvious and when the values it mimics are considered, rightly or wrongly, to belong to the very highest level of art, thought or emotion" (*NG,* 64, 67–68).

So years before achieving the tranquil well-being of *Ada,* Nabokov had punished Humbert at the expense of innocent (but "lowbrow") Lolita, depriving her of a small, ordinary life (but life nonetheless) in which family members call each other "honey," "baby," and "sweetheart." Having torn Dolly from her suburban childhood through Humbert's sexual obsessions, the author then returns her to a small life, giving her in marriage to the kind and deaf Dick Schiller and relegating her to the outskirts of Hunter Street. Unable to bear life's triviality, so unworthy of what "highbrow" beauty is supposed to be—pictures of Merimée's Carmencita or Botticelli's Venus—he finally kills her off in Gray Star, a distant northwestern settlement. Nabokov naturally attributes the comparison with Carmencita and Venus to Humbert, but it wasn't Humbert who executed little Dolores Haze: rather, her creator decides she's too good for this life and—despite her vulgar past—full of hopes which don't come true, corroded by the new vulgarity of Hunter Street or an Alaskan village.

Here's what became of the young aristocrat's first love—
Polenka—in *Speak, Memory:*

> . . . she and another girl walked past me, heavily ker-
> chiefed, in huge felt boots and horrible, shapeless, long
> quilted jackets, with the stuffing showing at the torn
> spots of the coarse black cloth, and as she passed,
> Polenka, a bruise under her eye and a puffed-up lip (did
> her husband beat her on Saturdays?), remarked in wist-
> ful and melodious tones to nobody in particular: *A
> barchuk-to menya ne priznal* [Look, the young master
> does not know me]. (*SM*, 165)

Lolita doesn't deserve such an ordinary fate!

And yet without forgiving Lolita's tormentor, Humbert, for
her nightmare childhood, we celebrate Lolita's real murderer,
Nabokov, for this crazy novel, grateful to him for her ultimate
salvation—the magnificent scene in Coalmont.

Humbert has come running at the call of Dolly, who is now
married and expecting a child: "Dear Dad, . . . Write, please. I
have gone through much sadness and hardship" (*Lolita*, 266).

> "You are sure you are not coming with me?"
> "No," she said. "No, *honey*, no."
> She had never called me honey before. (ibid., 279; my
> emphasis)

Honey—that one word is worth their whole romance; per-haps, it's worth the entire novel:

> In her washed-out gray eyes, strangely spectacled, our poor
> romance was for a moment reflected, pondered upon, and
> dismissed like a dull party, like a rainy picnic to which only
> the dullest bores had come, like a humdrum exercise, like
> a bit of dry mud caking her childhood. (ibid., 272)

Honey—this one word is a dismissal of the customary Russian "high" drama that overwhelms all aspects of our lives. *Honey* is not vulgarity but a human beauty rare for Nabokov. Humbert—*Dad*—whatever sort of monster he appears to the reader, is still dear to Lolita. Nabokov probably felt something similar toward Russia—it had disowned, abandoned, and betrayed him, but was still his native land.

Not the bad temper of a young nymphet, not her stays in American motels in a maniac's hands, but her capacity for kind-ness and forgiveness, in spite of all she'd been through, her inno-cent dream of a "normal" life, though banal and commonplace, at the edge of the world, in Alaska, in Gray Star, make Lolita, who dies giving birth to a stillborn girl, immortal.

Lolita is a novel about kindness. Kindness is immortal, espe-cially when it's a kindness that breaks through hurt and injustice. Lolita gathered what she could of her life from the fragments Humbert left her, and forgave her tormentor.[79] As for Nabokov, he was finally able to overcome that "Gogolian," very persistent Russian conviction that the human "median"[80] is an obvious vulgarity, an incarnation of the "eternal and universal evil" of banality. By allowing Lolita, not Venus or Carmencita, but ordinary, commonplace Lolita, to be lovely and loving he proved that *poshlost* is not always *poshlost*. It is "normalcy," and can indeed be loved.

"I shall never regret *Lolita*," said Nabokov. "She was like the composition of a beautiful puzzle—its composition and its solution at the same time, since one is a mirror view of the other, depending on the way you look. . . . There is a queer, tender charm about that mythical nymphet" (*SO*, I#3, 20–21). Not for nothing did he translate her into Russian: "in compensation, in a spirit of justice to my little American muse" (ibid., 37). Having solved this puzzle, Nabokov himself forgave Russia, his own Humbert: "it was not the Russia I remembered, but the factual Russia of today, forbidden to me, hopelessly slavish, and hopelessly my own native land" (VM, 285).

Nabokov empathized with Mandelshtam, loved Cincinnatus, spared Adam Krug suffering by plunging him into madness, and before rescuing Lolita from banality for eternity, rewarded her with kindness. Though distant and cold, Nabokov was nonetheless compassionate and sympathetic.

And here is another proof of his artistic kindness: he created Pnin—an even more generous authorial gesture, his finest. Nabokov rewarded Timofey Pnin, the heir of Cincinnatus and Mandelshtam, not for his strength, power, or talent but for his goodness. His gift to this hero isn't the poetic glory of Mandelsh-tam, or the posthumous peace of brave Cincinnatus, or the roman-tic happiness of Ada and Van Veen, but instead life and comfort, unlimited opportunity to graze on books (the greatest gift to a Russian intellectual), the relish of library life at Wordsmith University, in *this* world, in New Wye, Appalachia, USA.

Nabokov gives calm and courage to the remarkable Pnin, the most modern of Russian heroes: Pnin dares to live in the present, to dream and to lose, to fall and to rise—all the time remaining kind in the rational world of real, dreary, unromantic, unheroic, everyday misfortunes.

Though he has accepted the cold Western creed "Every man for himself," Pnin does not renounce the communal Russian "Vsyakii pred vsemi za vsekh vinovat"—"every one of us is an-swerable for everyone else"[81] (Dostoevsky's nineteenth-century formula was still applicable to all twentieth-century Russian liter-ature). Pnin remains our national treasure, the best proof of Nabokov's humanity. The author allowed Pnin to be better than him. Pnin isn't smarter, more successful, more heroic, or happier than his creator—simply *better*. Pronouncing life to be a tragic riddle, a "wallpaper" pattern that can't be solved logically, wise Pnin has learned the main lesson of life—the brave acceptance of our helplessness: "He was beloved not for any essential ability but for those unforgettable digressions of his, when he would remove his glasses to beam at the past while massaging the lenses of the present" (*Pnin*, 365).

It's for just such genuinely helpless smiles that we love Gogol and Chekhov, and we often reproach Dostoevsky for their absence. (To be fair, those smiles could be found in Dostoevsky too; the difference is that his—in Nabokov's and my opinion—are not signs of genuine vulnerability, instead they are tools, techniques, pieces of narrative construction that serve to support his mostly unfulfilled, although maybe brilliantly formulated, prophesies.)

Pnin—pathetic, unnecessarily robust-shouldered, big-hearted, comical, suffering, generous, brave Pnin—by nature is no hero. Sunk in the digressions, flourishes, circles and twists of Russian literature, Pnin mixes up his schedule, adapting poorly to American superficiality. He can't distinguish between what's commercial in America from what's cultural or humorous. Pnin's a Russian *intelligent*, not an American professor. "If his Russian was music, his English was murder" (*Pnin*, 409–10), the author explains. And, in classic Russian style, Pnin has an infinite "sympathy with failure" (ibid., 384). What makes him different, however, is that he is only "attached to his past but no longer hampered by it."[82]

"'In two-three years,' said Pnin, missing one bus but boarding the next, 'I will also be taken for an American'" (*Pnin*, 385), imagining in anticipation how he will dissolve among other professorial Wasps—with his new artificial teeth, artificial suntan, sunglasses, sneakers and other attributes that in a foreign mind mythologically constitute a perfect American. Of course, as Russian as he is—romantic, emotional, impractical, *Englishless*—he is already a perfect American—one of many diverse middle-class, driven individuals who compose, and ultimately get dissolved in, this cosmopolitan society.

Nabokov makes Pnin an American by placing his hero into a small life, forcing him to live as people live, day to day, without derring-do, refusing to see in suffering a sign of a higher spiritual design or an ultimate salvation. Nabokov closes the book on Dostoevsky, who, in Nabokov's view, is "venerate[d] [by most Russians] as a mystic and not as an artist. He was a prophet, a claptrap journalist, and a slapdash comedian" (*SO*, I#3, 42).

Dostoevsky's force and attraction for Russians lay precisely in the fact that he made the highest spiritual sense of the murders and perversions of all his Nastasiya Filipovnas and Rogozhins (*The Brothers Karamazov*), his Raskolnikovs, and his Stavrogins (*The Devils*): according to Dostoevsky, "the whole law of human existence is that a man should always be able to bow down before what's immeasurably great."[83] So, sin as much as you like, but don't neglect your faith, for with faith you can be forgiven everything.

In the Western world happiness isn't faith but *patience*, as *Pnin*'s author reminds us. It's not the meek, patient resignation of Russian literature that every so often impatiently explodes into revolutions and heroic deeds, but rather Western evolutionary perseverance: happiness is progress forward, and you need to create it yourself. Timofey Pnin refuses the patronage of an old acquaintance, an overwhelmingly successful Russian compatriot (evidently Nabokov himself), and courageously drives off into the future. In *Pale Fire,* which appeared two novels later, persevering and courageous Pnin is finally coming into his own, now saved not by Nabokov's artistic double, not even so much by a godlike creator himself, but by a virtue of being a hard-working American: Pnin gets a chair at Wordsmith University and a library to thrill any Russian intellectual. Even his ragged little white dog, acquired at some point in Waindell, has grown round and happy in New Wye.

For the nineteenth century it was Akaky Akakievich Bashmachkin, the timid clerk of Gogol's "Overcoat," who was the prototype of the Russian protagonist; his complaint "Why do you torment me?" was a standard refrain for the Russian hero. But the age of modernity—the twentieth century—left little charm in maladjustment, weakness, and defeatism to his successors, Anton Chekhov's heroes (and even Kafka's "Western" Gregor Samsa, who Nabokov insisted was also "very Gogolian" [*LOL*, 255]).[84] In contrast to the traditional plaintive suffering of Akaky Akakievich, their suffering was already tragic, requiring concrete relief, not murky spirits, ghostly flights, hallucinations, and apparitions.

When Nabokov calls both Akaky Akakievich and Gregor equally "pathetic," he is using the English word in its most negative sense—to connote "wretched," "dismal," "pitiable," "weak," "useless," "feeble." We encounter the word in *Pnin* as well: "pathetic savant" (385) is the phrase Pnin's landlords use to describe their endearing tenant. But in the narrator's eyes, Pnin, setting out for a "repulsive operation" to get new dentures, is quite "heroic" (ibid., 383, 386). Here, both "pathetic" and "heroic" are subjective, nonbinding judgments, applied to lodging arrangements or slightly shameful oral surgery. In Russian literature, pity and wretchedness had always been on a par with love and daring (in dying senselessly, pitiful Akaky Akakievich, unjustly deprived of his new overcoat, rebels heroically in spirit). But Pnin, that transitional mutant of time and geography, adapts pragmatically to his plastic teeth: he "began to enjoy his new gadgets. It was a revelation, it was a sunrise, it was a firm mouthful of efficient, alabastrine, humane America" (ibid., 387).

Overcoats and dentures are equally banal! But while Bashmachkin can break free of banality's gravity only through death and rebellion, a century later it is banality itself that brings happiness and inspiration to Pnin: "The great work on Old Russia, a wonderful dream mixture of folklore, poetry, social history, and *petite histoire,* which for the last ten years or so he had been fondly planning, now seemed accessible at last, with headaches gone, and this new amphitheater of translucid plastics implying, as it were, a stage and a performance" (*Pnin*, 387).

With Pnin's help, Nabokov has succeeded in leading the Russian hero out of the Chekhovian cul-de-sac—suffering without release in an enchanted cherry orchard. A Chekhovian Pnin, like the three sisters, would be trying to get to Moscow to this day. Nabokov's Pnin, on the other hand, leaves proudly for unpredictable uncertainty to realize his old continental dreams—"With grateful surprise, Pnin thought that there had been no Russian revolution, no exodus, no expatriation in France, no naturalization in America, everything—at the best, at the best, Timofey!—would have been much the same: a professorship in Kharkov or Kazan, a suburban house such as this, old books within, late blooms without" (*Pnin*, 473)—later on a different continent, in a different novel.

The difference between Timofey and Akaky Akakievich is that the old, communal Russian notion that the "little man" survives because he shares with others some ineffable quality of the national spirit[85] has been displaced by a new individuality that compels the heroic type to make it on his own, for himself, against all odds, by whatever means he alone can invent and endure.

After all, even the Russian language, which created and defined the non–"Protestant ethic" culture of Akaky Akakievich, Gogol, and Chekhov, won't answer for itself: impersonal constructions—*mne skuchno* (it's boring to me)—suggest that it is not I—Poprishchin, Ranevskaya, Gaev,[86] Belikov, Ivanov—that am responsible for my feelings and my life. For example, Pavel Ivanovich Chichikov and other characters of Gogol's *Dead Souls* are never in control of their fate. Driven by universal forces, life happens to them without their involvement or understanding. The Russian *ya* understands itself as an *object* of action, not a subject. But English "I" defines its own destiny in accordance with the Protestant ethic motto that no empowerment is as effective as self-empowerment.

It's no wonder that "I" is a mark of dangerous individuality—
Bend Sinister—in the uniform land of Paduk, where in Leninist-
Stalinist-Ekwilist style all must obey the motto proclaimed for
them: "all men consist of the same twenty-five letters variously
mixed" (*BS*, 68). Paduk, who has inherited Fradrik Skotoma's theory of Ekwilism—"balance as a basis for universal bliss" (ibid.,
75)—does not recognize "I," the capital letter of the Latin alphabet, and the most important English letter for defining *my*
individuality.

Adam Krug lived by that letter, and not only because, like
Nabokov, he was an indivisible monist philosophically. To stand
apart in Padukgrad was an act of especial daring and protest, akin
to Cincinnatus's opacity among the obediently translucent citizens of *Invitation to a Beheading* or Mandelshtam's enforced
silence in Stalin's Leningrad.

> I am a lake. I am a tongue. I am a spirit. I am fevered. I
> am not covetous. I am the Dark Cavalier. I am the torch.
> I arise. I ask. I blow. I bring. I cannot change. I cannot
> look. I climb the hill. I come. I dream. I envy. I found. I
> heard. I intended an Ode. I know. I love. I must not
> grieve, my love. I never. I pant. I remember. I saw thee
> once. I traveled. I wandered. I will. I will. I will. I will.
> (*BS*, 32)

In this single paragraph "I" is repeated thirty three times as a
sign of the human capacity for solitariness and individuality.

Pnin too evinces such individuality in his peculiar but fearless use of the English language: in this newly acquired means of expressing himself he "employs a nomenclature all his own. His verbal vagaries add a new thrill to life. His mispronunciations are mythopeic. His slips of the tongue are oracular" (*Pnin*, 491).

Nabokov maintained that artistic genius lay not in general ideas but in a certain way of seeing. As he wrote of Gogol, "His work, as all great literary achievements, is a phenomenon of language and not one of ideas" (*LOL*, 61).

If Akaky Akakievich is the prototype and precursor of Pnin, then Nabokov follows Gogol (with a stopover at Chekhov's) as just such a linguistic phenomenon. Russian was Sirin's worldview which required permanent modification. Thus, English with a capital "I" became Nabokov's. The change of languages predetermined the change in outlook—a linguistic phenomenon became a philosophical one.

The Russian-speaking Gogol and Chekhov stayed with their touching and trapped sufferers in the traditional nineteenth century. The transitional twentieth century tore brave, bewildered Mandelshtam to pieces. Nabokov's great heroes, the Europeans Martin Edelweiss, Cincinnatus C., and Adam Krug would share his tragic fate.

Nabokov himself has carried Russia into the future—the twenty-first century—into what Russia should one day become: a purposeful world of comfort, plastic, and successfully individualistic humanitarianism.[87] But generously, in the Russian way, he counterbalanced the indifference of democracy with his greatest heroes, heroes of kindness: Dolores Haze and Timofey Pnin. It is for them that we read and love Nabokov.

Epilogue:

Nabokov as the Pushkin

of the Twenty-first Century

A work of art teaches nothing—yet it teaches everything.
—Abram Tertz, *A Voice from the Chorus*

Nabokov surely would have liked this comparison with Pushkin. "Pushkin's blood runs through the veins of modern Russian literature," he once wrote (*SO*, I#6, 63). Pushkin was the only writer whose work Nabokov commented on but didn't rewrite, improve, or correct. But to which Pushkin should Nabokov be compared? Pushkin is versatile, light, a darling of all audiences, universal and lovingly familiar. He looks at us "from both sides at the same time . . . from above, from the side, from some third point of view."[1]

Here is one Pushkin, the Pushkin of "The Prophet," known to every Russian schoolchild:

Arise, O prophet, hark and see . . .
And, going over Land and Sea,
Burn human hearts with your Word.

Or here is another Pushkin, from "To a Poet," distant and solitary:

A poet! Do not prize the love of people around,
It soon will pass—the glorifying hum—
And come a court of fools and laughing of cold crowd—
But you must always stay firm, morose and calm.[2]

And here is one more, alone, self-centered and carefree, in "From Pindemonti" (1836) in Nabokov's own translation:

To give account to none, to be one's own
Vassal and lord, to please oneself alone, . . .
To stroll in one's own wake, admiring the divine
Beauties of nature and to feel one's soul
Melt in the glow of man's inspired design—
That is the blessing, those are the rights. (*LORL*, 12)

Nabokov, on the other hand, is *always* unapproachable—"I pride myself on being a person with no public appeal"; arrogant—"Let us look for the individual genius" (*LORL*, 11); alone and lonely—"I am interested in the lone performance" (*SO*, I#9, 117); difficult—"Art is difficult. Easy art is what you see at modern exhibitions of things and doodles" (ibid., 115). Nabokov favored common sense over rhyming beauty; he switched his writing from wordy, lengthy Russian to precise and sensible English. He preferred his own uneasy deceptions of many masks to the light, multifaceted nature of Pushkin: Pushkin organically, almost "vampirically" is turning into what he is describing, Nabokov only changes his masks while always remaining himself.

So which Pushkin should we choose when talking about Nabokov for twenty-first century Russia—a prophet, a poet, or a carefree artist? In his introduction to the *Lectures on Russian Literature* Nabokov undoubtedly chooses "From Pindemonti" as an example of his own type of "individual genius." Driving the reader out of his memoirs, barricading himself behind miles of ocean, the academic bubble, audiotaped lectures, Swiss neutrality, prefaces, afterwords, and the impenetrable cardboard of book covers, Nabokov guarded himself from any human contact—no trespassing! "The best reader," he asserted, "is an egotist, who takes pleasure in his treasures hiding from the neighbors" (PPP, 546).

His whole life Nabokov defended his image as an anticommunal writer:

Sometimes it may have been that even the most irreproachable artist tried to say his word in defense of the dying and miserable, but one should not give into this temptation, because we can be sure, if the cause requires suffering, it will die and will later bear unexpected fruit. No, definitely not; in the light of my lamp there is no place for the so-called social life and all the rest, which once pushed my compatriots to rebel. And if I don't ask for an ivory tower for myself, it is only because I am satisfied with my attic. (PPP, 550)

He fought for his freedom not to serve as a model—"a work of art has no importance whatever to society"—rejecting a prophetic calling for artists.

But in trying to convince us that his novels "have no moral message; no general ideals to exploit," that he simply "like[s] composing riddles with elegant solutions," Nabokov nonetheless slips: "A good combination [in chess, as in art] should always contain a certain element of deception" (*SO*, I#2, 12). And if we read carefully between the lines, look backstage, study the backdrop behind his endless masks (going, of course, against the writer's will, but also following his own encouragement, "In reading, one should notice and fondle details" [*LOL*, 1]), we will assertively discover that he is indeed Pushkin's Prophet—"Burn human hearts with your Word."

Working tirelessly on his language and style—"I have rewritten—often several times—every word I have ever published" (*SO*, I#1, 4), strategically displaying his endless traps of riddles, puzzles, charades, tricks, and mirror reflections, Nabokov was addressing not his Western contemporaries or even his Russian counterparts but us in the future, "The real writer should ignore all readers but one, that of the future, who in turn is merely the author reflected in time."

"Of all the characters that a great artist creates, his readers are the best," he insisted, adding with a hope, "the Russian reader . . . seems to me to be as much of a model for readers as Russian writers were models for writers in other tongues. He would start on his charmed career at a most tender age and lose his heart to Tolstoy and Chekhov when still in the nursery" (*LORL*, 11).

Therefore, we, those Russian readers of Nabokov who after Tolstoy and Chekhov finally have been able to study his belatedly, but timely, published works, we choose to courageously disagree with the writer, who wanted us to believe in his mask of disdain, indifference, unsociability, and unkindness.

Russian literature (and here we agree with Nabokov) is indeed an example to all other literatures. In fact, it is an example of that which Nabokov so resented in it—spiritual leadership. Spirit, soul is our greatest national achievement as well as our great national handicap: "We may be backward, but we have souls." With this comforting Dostoevskian maxim Russians usually console themselves for their lack of products, laws, and services.

"The most important quality of a Russian is that he feels he has nothing to lose. Thus, the Russian *intelligent* is disinterested and selfless (save for his bookshelf)," [3] say philosophers to explain our impracticality and nonmaterialism. Hence writers in Russia become the "vlastiteli dum" (owners of thoughts) of our spirit and soul. They are the guides and the prophets. Often, their "burning" brings rather horrific results: in accordance with Lenin's famous remark "In Memory of Herzen," "The Decembrists aroused

Herzen, who then started revolutionary propaganda."[4] Then came Chernyshevsky, then Maxim Gorky, and finally the whole of Russia ended up in the gulag. But this only proves the point—a poet in Russia is more than just a poet.

Disagreeing with Dostoevsky on this very idea of soulful backwardness, Nabokov had his own answer to *The Brothers Karamazov*'s celestial formula that "every one of us is answerable for everyone else" (the exact translation is "we are all each for each other guilty"): "My indifference to religion is of the same nature as my dislike of group activities in the domain of political or civic commitments" (*SO*, I#4, 48). Nabokov didn't feel guilty and wanted to remain a Russian, but there were other more practical Karamazovs, such as Lenin & Co., who out of the typical guilt of the Russian intelligentsia toward the "oppressed masses" decided to construct a bright future for the whole of humanity, thus curing it of all possible guilt. In extreme revolutionary zeal they of course overdid it, constructing instead of a bright future a "prison of nations," where all have become guilty for not being guilty enough—quite a banal historical paradox.

And then Nabokov, who always rejected any form of group therapy—"It is nothing but a kind of microcosmos of communism—all that psychiatry. . . . Why not leave their private sorrows to people? Is sorrow not, one asks, the only thing in the world people really possess?" (*Pnin*, 398)—declared outright that he no longer wanted to be a Russian. He had to survive in a new reality of non-Russianness, in the uncomfortable conditions of the rational, linear world, where the image of the suffering artist is devoid of any romanticism; where the highly spiritual weakness of an *intelligent*, so well described by Chekhov, is far from being a virtue; where each is responsible for oneself. In that world romantic ideas and utopian philosophies, despite their Western origins, were wisely not put into practice, but comfortably left to turn yellow in the pages of old books.

Claiming to be an absolutely American writer, who simply happened to have been born in Russia, Nabokov, whether he wanted to admit it or not, had still been brought up in the traditions of Russian culture, in the traditions of the Poet as national treasure, destined "to extol kind feelings with his lyre."[5] And thus, despite himself, he passionately believed in the material, physical power of the word. But a new word—pointed and cogent, in which the "passion of science" should be combined with the "patience of poetry" (*SO*, I#1, 7).

In the "Russian" period of his emigration Nabokov simply tried out Western writers, and sharpened his Russian style, to make it more suitable to a new modern—a more "linear"—hero. "A very bothersome feature that Russian presents is the dearth, vagueness, and clumsiness of technical terms," he complained. His brand of clear and cloudless Russian was supposed to replace the country's linguistic tradition of baroque metaphor with "functional imagery" (*SM*, 225) and precise, almost mathematically calculated comparison. E. T. A. Hoffman's gargoyles and doppelgangers in *The Eye* and *Despair*, Shakespeare's Hamlet themes in *Mary* and *Glory* are still understood through the prism of Russian literature—Nikolai Gogol and Andrei Bely.[6] But unlike his Russian predecessors Nabokov already at that time made clear attempts to create a new victorious and rational, efficiently Western character, free from Russian impractical reflections and doubts, high feelings and multi-meanings, ethereal thoughts and dreams so familiar to us from Goncharov, Dostoevsky, Tolstoy, and Chekhov. This protagonist's own life, often in the form of simple survival, is more important to him than the all-encompassing, world-loving, and nonmaterial ideals of Russian literature. Ganin in *Mary*, Martin in *Glory*, Godunov-Cherdyntsev in *The Gift*—all of them care more for their own personal convenience than for some utopian common good, and have no qualms about doing so.

Instead of never-ending forests, woods, and cherry orchards that would eventually be toppled by some post-Chekhovian revolutionary, Nabokov preferred to grow solitary, thorny cactuses.

Before him, Russian literature didn't have a prickly "Western" hero, didn't have an "individual genius" similar to Nabokov himself, grossly self-absorbed and driven by his own personal interests, in accord with Adam Smith's utilitarian notion that it is the individual ambition that serves the common good.

Until Nabokov our individualistic characters like Onegin and Pechorin, the so-called "outcast men," as poetic as they were, were also "otritsatelnye geroi" (negative heroes), that is, they were uniformly criticized for destroying life around them, not creating it.

Until Nabokov, even "Western" types in Russian literature such as Ivan Turgenev's Insarov, a Bulgarian from *On the Eve* (1860),[7] considered their social calling more important than their lonely ambitions.

And while Alexander Blok's and Sergei Yesenin's imagery was also about solitude, it was a solitude from which they suffered romantically.[8] Marina Tsvetaeva echoed them from her Paris emigration, "If voice is given to you, Poet, the rest is taken away."[9]

Before Pushkin there was no Russian literature in its contemporary sense, that is, there were odes, ballads, poems, but no short stories, novels, lyrical poems: "All themes . . . were accessible to him, and running through them, he marked out roads for Russian letters for centuries to come. No matter where we poke our noses—Pushkin is everywhere, which can be explained not so much by the influence of his genius on other talents, as by the fact that there isn't a motif in the world he didn't touch upon. Pushkin simply managed to write about everything for everyone."[10]

In the same way today many Russians, some still unwillingly, find themselves reflected in Nabokov's many characters, dispersed throughout his many novels and stories as "people, wearing [their author's] own mask." More than half a century in advance he predicted our destiny for us. Keeping his usual mask of careless disdain, Nabokov created a new Russia with the elegant and happy solution for its problems (*Ada* is the final outcome), "We should always remember that the work of art is invariably the creation of a new world" (*LOL*, 1).

"Sower of freedom in the desert, I started before the stars came out,"[11] Nabokov could have repeated after Pushkin. We, the watchers and readers of Russia, would say it for him. Following the writer's experience, fully in the spirit of Nabokovian infinity—the continuation of thematic design, a pattern that has turned out to be yet another coil in the eternal spiral—his heroes forestalled Russia's own post-Soviet fate. Cincinnatus, like all of us, had to crawl out of the lazy consciousness of Russian literature, out of Ilya Ilyich Oblomov, who finally had to get up, take off his robe, make decisions, and become Andrei Shtoltz.

The fact that we, unlike Nabokov who considered his pre-emigration life ideal, wanted Western, calculated order in our own irrational land and strove to exchange the languid Oblomov for the enterprising Shtoltz, did not ease our apprehensive transition from "human" (*chelovecheskii*—personal, emotional humanism) to "humane" (*gumannyi, chelovechnyi*—rational, individualistic humanitarianism), our awkward adjustment to the cruel, measured, hollow, and unforgiving laws of capitalism, in which only the strongest survive. This situation simply stresses the subordination of reality to eternity: Luzhin, Cincinnatus C., Pnin, Kinbote, Van Veen, and Ada will remain figments of artistic imagination in their immortality as their suffering is over, while we must live on in the transitional period from socialism to capitalism, totalitarianism to democracy, spiritual values to material ones, all-encompassing nature to rationality, from the twentieth century to the twenty-first.

How to survive in "normalnoi, tsivilizovannoi strane" (a normal, reasonable, civilized country), without the option of running away, jumping out of oneself, with no Troika Bird salvation of dreams and spirituality; how to learn to live "kak lyudi zhivut" (like people live), day by day, evolutionarily, not revolutionarily, routinely and ordinarily, without thinking about some utopian bright future that somebody will build for us; having no other choice than "razumnyi egoizm" (rational selfishness),[12] not in the form of the useless tenacity of Chernyshevsky, whom Nabokov laughed at in *The Gift*, but as a self-protective coldness, self-sufficiency, and distance from all, is taught to us by the most insensitive and unsympathetic, most compassionate and caring modern writer in Russia today.

Nabokov once joked, "I believe that one day a reappraiser will come and declare that, far from having been a frivolous firebird, I was a rigid moralist kicking sin, cuffing stupidity, ridiculing the vulgar and cruel—assigning sovereign power to tenderness, talent and pride" (*SO*, I#19, 193). In saying this he recognized himself as a Prophet.

The End

So why do we happily forgive Gogol for his paranoia, Pushkin for his wild ways, Tolstoy for his habitual proselytizing, and Dostoevsky for his violent humility (*yurodivshchina*), but are unwilling to forgive Nabokov for his vanity and airs? Why, in the cases of Gogol, Pushkin, Tolstoy, and Dostoevsky do we patiently, willingly, generously separate human failings from artistic genius, but refuse to accord Nabokov anything like the same tolerance? Why does Nabokov's personality seem to so rub us the wrong way? Of course, we admire the style, the wit, the heroes, the strength, and the talent, yet we sometimes discount all of that and remain outraged by the sheer unmitigated arrogance of the man.

Is our intolerance due to the fact that only thirty years have passed since Nabokov's death? Because there are still people around who were at the receiving end of his barbs and jibes, while Pushkin, Gogol, Tolstoy, and Dostoevsky, like the monuments they are, have had their human characteristics worn away, eroded, by time?

Perhaps it's because Nabokov, like no other writer, while insisting on purging his works of anything remotely personal, refuses at the same time to let the reader lose sight of him for a minute. He once claimed that "what ideas can be traced in my novels belong to my creatures therein and may be deliberately flawed. In my memoirs, quotable ideas are merely passing visions, suggestions, mirages of the mind. They lose their colors and explode like football fish when lifted out of the context of their tropical sea" (*SO*, I#13, 147)—a clear warning not to think we could ever "know him"—his thoughts and characters—by reading his books. In his writings, Nabokov the man is invisible yet recognizable in every word and phrase, a deity guiding the narrative to ensure the needed effect: "there has been one . . . it is hard to express it . . . a nameless, mysterious genius who took advantage of the dream to convey his own peculiar code message" (*BS*, 64).

So we get endless translations, prefaces, postscripts, and commentaries to his novels—just in case, God forbid, there's something we didn't catch. No other author so mocks us, derides us, meddles with our reading of his books, his heroes, his own self. It's hard, if not impossible, to forgive him for our repeated humiliations and discomfort.

Or perhaps we are unforgiving of Nabokov because he seems

so petty in his likes and dislikes; so arbitrary, categorical, and aggressive in his biases; so smug, finding fault with practically everyone, living and dead: their personal shortcomings, their literary shortcomings. It's hard to accept that a real genius must be so painfully anxious about his own gifts that he feels the need to belittle the gifts of everyone else. Although the following quote from Khodasevich supposedly builds a case for Nabokov, it actually works against him: "a poet tries to conceal his genius. Thus, Pushkin covered it with the mask of a gambler, the cloak of a duelist, the patrician robe of an aristocrat, the bourgeois jacket of a literary dealer. On the other hand, a person without talent always tries to promote his alleged specialty as a simulator-beggar exposes his sores."[1] And God knows—Nabokov *does* try to promote himself. It is as if he plays the crafty, conspiratorial Salieri to Pushkin's innocent Mozart.

Yet reading Nabokov today, almost a half-century after he finished his great works, when the world tends to value advertisements more than art; when self-promotion is often considered a form of genius, it is unfair to deny Nabokov his true rank among the great simply because he was a truly modern writer, taking credit for his artistic miracles and mirages, putting no stock in heavenly blessings. In our modern global world, talent can't rely on the usual Russian *avos da nebos* (the off-chance probability); on somehow flourishing after being left to the mercy of fate. The erratic Mozart may still inspire, but he is no longer a role model for artists. Careless about his talent, he wouldn't have lasted a day in today's McArtist's world; more likely, he would have wound up as a busker playing for pennies on the Schubertring, the Arbat, or Broadway, rather than the Musikvereinssaal, the Moscow Conservatory, or Carnegie Hall. No, nowadays it's the industrious and "goal-oriented" Salieris, the people who give interviews to *People* magazine and are profiled in the *New York Times,* who make it to the top in the art racket. Nabokov understood his times: he is Salieri, pushing his way ahead not with poison but with a stinging pen. Today, Salieri is Mozart.[2] Nabokov is today's Pushkin.

Or maybe it's because we ourselves, ordinary people, still cling to a traditional sense of divine justice, despite the growing pragmatism of our times. We're happy to see hubris punished. Americans are fond of the phrase, "Nobody likes a smartass," despite—or precisely because of—the fact that most of them (to my mind) dream of being just such a smartass, outpacing their rivals and affirming a different truth—that "good guys finish last." But the durable concepts of the centuries-long not-always-so-affirmative non-Protestant ethic continue to linger in the background of my Russian Orthodox autocratic consciousness: creatures of flesh and blood ought not to believe themselves on a par with the gods. All the other greats played by the rules, more than paying for their blessed talent: Pushkin, like a child, ridiculously, was killed in a duel; old Tolstoy died an unhappy and lonely death; Gogol was buried alive, and vanished slowly while watching worms crawl all over his face as it was growing cold. Horrible!

Nabokov alone emerged dry from the water onto other

shores. He lived not only to give evidence of his greatness in a book of memoirs, but also to add a postscript about just what makes that book so great. In short, he didn't pay any mortal price for his genius. It's unfair!

But all the same . . .

In accordance with the authorial principle of retrospective genius, Nabokov the man paid in full, simply in reverse order, in advance. Nabokov the boy lost his country, his home, his family, their Vyra estate, Saint Petersburg, his language—everything he loved—long before Nabokov the writer became a genius.

Envoi

In the very hot summer of 2003, fleeing a Paris steaming in tropical heat, I decided to visit Montreux again, to thank Nabokov for the fascinating years I had spent contemplating his thoughts and words, and to see whether I had got him right, whether he might want to correct something. I was nervous getting off the train, though I noted with some comfort—the new century has been rather unsettling—that the town hadn't changed much since my last time there, the year of the writer's centennial. Would he talk to me again? Did he remember me at all? Full of anticipation—once again Nabokov would sit before me in a bronze chair—I walked into the hotel lobby and took a few steps, only to freeze—Nabokov wasn't there.

The town hadn't changed, but the inside of the hotel had—its enormous, luxurious lobby was broken into little "intimate quarters"—a table here, a settee there, a lamp, a pair of chairs, another table, another chair . . .

My Russian mind, prone to an associative type of thinking (I try hard to keep it in check!), raced to speculate: traditional, that is, high-class, elite cosmopolitanism is no longer in vogue—today its democratized, mass market version is an everyday reality—and the Montreux Palace, which once took pride in being worldly and intercontinental, has paid its tribute to the new century, balancing its cool impersonality with a contrived and cozy illusion of manageability and intimacy. The Palace's divided spaces should make its savvy "new age" guests feel less small and vulnerable in an unpredictable twenty-first century. All this, of course, leaves little room for Nabokov's old-fashioned exclusive and aristocratic sophistication. Some guests must have felt uncomfortable, discovering that they were not as suave as they thought they were before ignorantly stumbling onto his standoffish statue.

But the statue was gone. I was calling on the true owner of the place, but the owner had been evicted. Perhaps, however, the change wasn't as complex as my intellectual Russianness tried to make it. What if the hotel had hired a new superintendent, who turned out to be even more indifferent than your usual Swiss? This person simply ordered the hotel to be redecorated in accord with what he or she thought better suited our contemporary tastes. Settees and chairs are more useful to the Montreux Palace's guests than an eccentric piece of bronze.

The concierge smiled politely, *"Ne vous inquiétez pas.* Nabokov is right there, across the street now." When I expressed my concern that he may not like to be outside, out of his sheltered hotel element, exposed to the coarse elements and oblivious passersby, the concierge was surprised: "It's really good for him, he has his own monumental space now." He went on to explain that a sculpture in a hotel is too limiting—unfit for a great writer; it's not significant enough, doesn't fully reflect his stature and magnitude.

I walked out and crossed Grand-Rue: in a little park (albeit a treeless one), a gated open space, in a bronze chair, slouching under the scorching sun, sat Nabokov.

In the hotel his bronze figure was a private matter, a stylish if slightly affected décor for refined visitors. There he retained his delicate, genuinely Nabokovian balance between home and homelessness (a hotel allows for both), the illusory existence and material nothingness, the humanity and immortality that were his true cares. Now silently sitting in plain view, in an open intersection of roads, verticals and horizontals, he has become a mere *obychnyi* (customary), canonized tribute to a dead author. He has entered inhuman, impersonal eternity like other greats before him, becoming indisputably public—like some forgotten general, to be looked at briefly or ignored.

But perhaps the concierge was right in a way—for eternity, Nabokov is better off under the collective sky: no longer a guest himself, on earth or in the hotel: he is set free. He has become part of the world (Russia's finally if not yet completely included) literary canon, irreproachable, indisputable . . . with no personal control (and no personal worries) over public memory (although, always true to himself, he will continue to argue the opposite on the pages of his books).

Moreover, similar to the monumental cases of Pushkin, Gogol, Tolstoy, or Dostoevsky, very soon, in another decade or two, no one will care about Vladimir Nabokov's thorny character—brave or dispassionate, compassionate or insufferable. It will acquire a mellow patina like his now bronze self. Over the years our private feelings of intimidation, dislike, or adoration will turn into common acknowledgment, respect, indifference, even ignorance— Whose statue is that? Nabokov. Who is Nabokov?—"Awful question: Who is this unfortunate Fulmerford?"

Following Nabokov's own predictions there will be some (or much) name recognition: "I have fair inkling of my literary afterlife. I have sensed certain hints, I have felt the breeze of certain promises. No doubt there will be ups and downs, long periods of slump. With the Devil's connivance, I open a newspaper of 2063 and in some article on the books page I find: 'Nobody reads Nabokov or Fulmerford today.'"

There will be inevitable sound bites: "I confess I do not believe in time" will travel hand in hand with another celebrated quote, "Ya pamyatnik sebe vozdvig nerukotvornyi" ("No hands have wrought my monument").

Released into public space a monument becomes a symbol of

personal forgetting, a slice of universal, collective memory—
we don't have to rely on our human remembrance as there is a
piece of stone, of metal, of clay, to safely store an image forever.
It is also a symbol of forgiveness of one's private humanity and
imperfection—a stone on grounds accessible to all is a step toward
our common humanity that the past shares with the future.[1]

I was happy—no one could ever doubt my hero's eternity: the
bronze Nabokov will forever sit facing the tranquil Lake Geneva
in Montreux. I was even happier—from now on our conversation
would remain my exclusive story: as a public monument he will
never hold a private meeting again; there was no salon for him to
receive guests, no music room to converse over tea about his past
and our future.

But I was sorry, very sorry—he was no longer *my* Nabokov,
the Nabokov who occasionally grants those meetings. I was sorry
the sun could not deepen his bronze, he would be rained and
snowed on, cold in the winter and hot in the summer. And I was
sorrier still that he wouldn't even know the difference—a dead
genius, a silent statue.

The fiery air finally started to cool off. The sun set, spangling
the lake, its last dying reflections glittered on the windows of the
Palace. It was time to say goodbye, to let him be, to leave . . .

But once again, I was no longer there.

Nabokov sat alone, bronze, still, indifferently gazing off to
the side, into eternity, the grand and brilliant Nabokov, author
of *Lolita* and *Speak, Memory*, *Onegin* and *Gogol*, *Ada* and *Pale*

Fire, the Nabokov who translated, rewrote, added forewords, commentaries, and indexes to his novels, the Nabokov who explained everything and revealed nothing, the Russian classic of the "American" century, forever immersed in his monumental exclusivity.[2]

Notes

Introduction. Nabokov and Us

1. Grigory Pechorin is a main character of *A Hero of Our Time* (1840) by Mikhail Lermontov. Pechorin, as well as the eponymous hero of Alexander Pushkin's *Eugene Onegin* (1825–32), is a classic example of the Russian individualistic "lishny chelovek" (outcast man), who combines a poetic soul with high contempt for the herd, thus assuming the mask of a snob and a bully.

2. The poetic career of Anna Akhmatova (1889—1966) in Saint Petersburg spanned over half a century. An author of many memorable lyric poems, she also wrote a long poem *Requiem* (1935–40), a masterly narrative on life in Stalinist Leningrad.

3. Dmitri Nabokov's blog, "The Beginning of the End," posted March 29, 2006; dmitrinabokov.blogspot.com/ (accessed December 16, 2006).

4. Adam Smith, *An Inquiry into the Nature and Causes of the Wealth of Nations,* ed. Edwin Cannan, vol. 4 (Chicago: University of Chicago Press, 1976), 208.

5. Andrei Sinyavsky, *Ivan-Durak: Ocherk russkoi narodnoi very* (Moscow: Agraf, 2001), 235.

6. See Isaiah Berlin, *Russian Thinkers* (London: The Hogarth Press, 1978).

7. Fyodor Dostoevsky, *The Diary of a Writer* (New York: George Braziller, 1954), 296–97.

8. As a rule Russia has made little distinction between Catholic and Protestant brands of Christianity, defining geography to the west of the Gulf of Finland as the general "West." In Russian eyes all Western cultures were too materialist—lacking soulful essence, they didn't revere the Holy Ghost, and thus were equally opposed to Orthodoxy, which represented the belief in spirit, soul, and material sacrifice. Even France, probably culturally closer to Russia than other Western European countries, was seen as too bourgeois, while Germany, from which Russia borrowed most of its philosophy, was considered too *poshlaya* (banal, trivial, trite, complacent, vulgar). Nabokov, in fact, refers to this Russian conceptualization of Germany's *poshlost* in his book on Nikolai Gogol (cf. chapter 2, note 29). Today, however,—not least due to the twentieth-century Cold War divide—it is the United States, the remaining superpower and now the mightiest global power, that mostly corresponds to the legendary "West," encompassing all evils and virtues it has ever represented to the Russians.

9. Max Weber, *The Protestant Ethic and the Spirit of Capitalism* (Los Angeles: Roxbury, 2002), 68.

10. Ibid., 160, 59, 61.

11. Andrei Sinyavsky, *Soviet Civilization: A Cultural History* (New York: Little, Brown–Arcade, 1990), 117.

12. A. S. Khomyakov, "O starom i novom," in *Russkaya ideya,* ed. M. A. Maslin (Moscow: Respublika, 1992), 58.

13. Quoted in Sinyavsky, *Soviet Civilization,* 120.

14. Weber, *The Protestant Ethic,* 75.

15. Konstantin Aksakov, *Sobranie sochinenii v dvukh tomakh* (Moscow, 1911), 1:291–292.

16. Quoted in Jochen Hellbeck, *Revolution on My Mind: Writing a Diary under Stalin* (Cambridge, Mass.: Harvard University Press, 2006), 5–6.

17. Sinyavsky, *Soviet Civilization*, 116.

18. Anatoly Chubais in a TV interview on the Russian program *Detali*, June 29, 1994.

19. Quotation from Alexander Herzen in K. Skalkovsky, ed., *Russkie o russkikh: Mneniya russkikh o samikh sebe* (1904; Saint Petersburg: Petro-Rif, 1992), 49.

20. See "Nigeria No. 1 in Happiness Survey," Reuters, October 2, 2003. Also see "Nigeria Tops Happiness Survey," BBC News, October 2, 2003; http://news.bbc.co.uk/2/hi/africa/3157570.stm (accessed November 11, 2003).

21. David Landes, "Culture Makes Almost All the Difference," in *Culture Matters: How Values Shape Human Progress*, ed. Lawrence E. Harrison and Samuel P. Huntington (New York: Basic Books, 2000), 11–12.

22. Andrei Sinyavsky was one of the most important Russian writers of the "Thaw" post-Stalin period. A promising young Soviet literary scholar, beginning in the late 1950s Sinyavsky started to send abroad—under the pseudonym Abram Tertz—writings that he could not publish legally in the Soviet Union. For these writings, which included a critically provocative piece "On Socialist Realism" (1957), he was arrested in 1965, tried in 1966, and sentenced to one of the infamous Soviet forced labor camps, Dubrovlag. In his five years of imprisonment he wrote, among other things, his best-known literary and philosophical works, *Strolls with Pushkin* (published in 1975 after his emigration to France in 1973) and *A Voice from the Chorus* (published in the year of his emigration). While teaching at the Sorbonne in the 1970s and 1980s he wrote a number of important socio-philosophical commentaries on Russia and its culture, including *Ivan the Fool: Essays on the Russian National Faith* and *Soviet Civilization*.

23. See Richard Pipes, "Flight From Freedom: What Russians Think and Want," *Foreign Affairs*, May/June 2004.

24. The complexity of reasons—from artistic to emotional to practical—for Nabokov's choice to abandon his native Russian is well detailed in Elizabeth Klosty Beaujour's book *Alien Tongues: Bilingual Russian Writers of the "First" Emigration* (Ithaca, N.Y.: Cornell University Press, 1989), 81–117.

25. The English "I" came to be capitalized in Middle English to help distinguish it as a separate word, to avoid being misread as just a letter in handwritten manuscripts. It first appeared in uppercase in Midland dialects of England in the mid-thirteenth century, though in the south the use of the original first-person form "ich" continued for much longer, until the eighteenth century. *Oxford English Dictionary*, 2d. ed., s.v. "I, pers. pron., 1st sing."

    My hypothesis is that although original capitalization of the English "I" happened for practical reasons it then could have fit excellently into the Anglo-Saxon individualistic culture that has become a worldview. Boris Gasparov, professor of Slavic languages at Columbia University, suggested in a private conversation that while this hypothesis defies scientific proof, it is entirely plausible. Capital "I" did indeed become a cultural phenomenon—the letter grew to signify not just the grammatical first person singular but also the individualistic spirit of a self-helping culture, now seen as something special to be associated with the Anglo-Saxon-American world of capitalism.

26. "Ya—poslednya bukva alfavita" ("'i' is the last letter of the alphabet")—is the principal expression that Russian children memorize while learning to read and write: our culture considers it ill mannered to make references to oneself when talking or writing to someone else. "Ya" is indeed the last letter of the Russian alphabet, and you can only imagine how damaging such a linguistic worldview could be to one's self-esteem.

27. Michael Scammell, "The Servile Path (Translating Vladimir Nabokov by Epistle)," *Harper's Magazine* 302 (May 2001): 57.

28. Weber, *The Protestant Ethic*, 62.

29. For references to "circular Russian literature" cf. chapter 1, note 32, and chapter 2, note 15. One could argue that some English novels

such as Laurence Sterne's *The Life and Opinions of Tristram Shandy, Gentleman* (1759–67), are also open-ended like Russian literary works. But as the Russian formalist critic Victor Shklovsky argued in his essay "The Novel as Parody: Sterne's *Tristram Shandy*": "This is of course a definite stylistic device based on differential qualities. Sterne was writing against a background of the adventure novel with its extremely rigorous forms that demanded, among other things, that a novel end with a wedding and marriage. The forms most characteristic of Sterne are those which result from the displacement and violation of conventional forms" (Victor Shklovsky, *Theory of Prose* [Elmwood Park, Ill.: Dalkey Archive Press, 1991], 156). In contrast, modern, i.e. post-eighteenth–century Russian literature, had no such "rigorous forms," and only in a very few (and very un-convincing instances) such as the patriarchal marriage of Natasha Rostova to Pierre Bezukhov at the end of Tolstoy's *War and Peace*, has an ending, let alone a happy one. In another work Shklovsky juxtaposed the British case of "violating the conventional norms" with a Russian norm of altogether dispensing with endings and happiness, equating it with a state of mind: "The greatness of Russian literature is in its ability not to create endings. Great literature doesn't know happy endings. . . . Happy endings are for a different humanity—a happy humanity. . . . Happy endings of the great English novels are false endings" (Viktor Shklovsky, *Energiya zabluzh-deniya: Kniga o syuzhete,* in Viktor Shklovsky, *Izbrannoe v dvukh tomakh* [Moscow: Khudozhestvennaya literatura, 1983], 2:388–89). Mikhail Bulgakov's open-ended novel *Master and Margarita* (1937) is a twentieth-century case in point.

Incidentally, another "definite stylistic device" in *Tristram Shandy* is that it lacks plot formation, which too is typical of Russian literature. But in the Russian case this "amorphousness" is a world-view rather than a question of style—in *A Voice from the Chorus* Abram Tertz has explained this Russian disregard for a conclusion, or a conventional plot, or genre in general as a cultural norm (cf. chapter 2, note 12). To cite a few examples, Nikolai Gogol's novel

Dead Souls (1842) is called a poem, Alexander Pushkin's poem *Eugene Onegin* is considered a novel, and Anton Chekhov's thoroughly dramatic, if not tragic, plays are titled "comedies."

30. "Vse my vyshli iz Gogolevskoi 'Shineli'" ("We have all come out of Gogol's 'Overcoat'") is a famous Russian saying usually attributed to Fyodor Dostoevsky. Akaky Akakievich Bashmachkin, a petty Saint Petersburg clerk, is a main character of Gogol's novella "The Overcoat" (1842).

31. Weber, *The Protestant Ethic*, 109.

32. Abram Tertz (Andrei Sinyavsky), *A Voice from the Chorus* (New York: Farrar, Straus and Giroux, 1976), 247.

33. Pushkin, "Poetu" ("To a Poet") (1830); translation by Yevgeny Bonver; www.poetryloverspage.com/poets/pushkin/to poet.html (accessed February 12, 2004). Pushkin is seen simultaneously as Russia's most Russian and most Western poet—he wrote pithily in French as well as Russian, and, in Nabokov's words, as "professional poet and Russian nobleman, used to shock the *beau monde* by declaring that he wrote for his own pleasure but published for the sake of money" (*SO*, I#13, 144).

34. Aleksandr Sergeevich Pushkin, *Stikhotvorenia* (Moscow: Khudozhestvennaya Literatura, 1985), 211; translation by Yevgeny Bonver; www.poetryloverspage.com/poets/pushkin/prophet.html (accessed February 12, 2004).

35. Simon Karlinsky, "Nabokov and Chekhov: the Lesser Russian tradition," in *Nabokov: Criticism, Reminiscences, Translations and Tributes*, ed. Alfred Appel Jr. and Charles Newman (London: Weidenfeld and Nicolson, 1970), 8.

36. Ilya Ilyich Oblomov—hero of Ivan Goncharov's novel *Oblomov* (1859). The landowner Oblomov is considered the epitome of Russian laziness, patience, kindness, and compassion.

37. Brian Boyd, *Vladimir Nabokov: The American Years* (Princeton, N.J.: Princeton University Press, 1991), 475.

38. Quoted in Karlinsky, "Nabokov and Chekhov," 8.

Prologue. Nabokov's Russian Return . . . and Retreat

1. See Edward T. Hall, *Beyond Culture* (New York: Anchor Press, 1976); E. T. Hall and M. R. Hall, *Understanding Cultural Differences* (Yarmouth, Maine: Intercultural Press, 1990); and Susanne Niemeir, Charles P. Campbell, and Rene Dirven, eds., *The Cultural Context in Business Communication* (Philadelphia: John Benjamin, 1998).

The general terms "high-context" and "low-context" are used to describe cultural differences between societies. "High-context" refers to societies or groups where people have close connections over a long period of time. Many aspects of cultural behavior are not made explicit because most members know what to do and what to think from years of interaction with each other (hence their "circular," "associative" way of thinking, brought about by many assumed implicit connections). A family (or a Russian commune, for that matter) is an example of a high-context environment. "Low-context" refers to societies where people tend to approach life in sequential terms. They too have many connections but of shorter duration or for some specific reason. In these societies, cultural behavior and beliefs may need to be spelled out explicitly so that those coming into the cultural environment know how to behave.

Behaviors that define high-context cultures are dense, consist of intersecting networks and long-term relationships, strong boundaries, and the belief that relationship as more important than task. These cultures don't value formal written information; instead they prefer decisions and activities that require face-to-face communication, often around a central person in a position of authority. For low-context cultures loose, wide networks and shorter-term, compartmentalized relationships are more typical. They are rule-oriented, i.e. people play by external rules and value knowledge that is explicit, accessible, and consciously organized. Tasks and goals are altogether more important than relationships, which provides for "linear," sequential thinking.

2. Mike Eckel, "Putin Calls Collapse of Soviet Union 'Catastrophe,'" Associated Press, April 25, 2005.

3. Arkady Ostrovsky, "Gazprom Acts as Lever in Putin's Power Play," *Financial Times,* March 13, 2006; news.ft.com/cms/s/8c1e9dca b2cc-11da-ab3e-0000779e2340.html (accessed March 14, 2006).

4. President Vladimir Putin's opening address at meeting with G8 finance ministers, February 11, 2006; my emphasis; www.kremlin.ru/eng/speeches/2006/02/11/1400_type82914_101549.shtml (accessed November 15, 2006).

5. Russia holds 13 percent of the world's oil reserves, and about 34 percent of the world's natural gas. G8 partners of Russia—Britain, France, Germany, and Italy—as well as the other EU countries currently receive more than 60 percent of Russia's output of oil and gas. All in all, twenty-five European countries import from Russia 50 percent of their gas and 30 percent of their oil. See Artur Blinov, "Report: Energeticheskii dialog na fone politicheskogo krizisa," *Nezavisimaya Gazeta,* March 1, 2006.

6. "Polls & Research: Russia's Putin Maintains Impressive Numbers," Angus Reid Global Monitor, October 6, 2006; www.angus-reid .com/polls/index.cfm/fuseaction/viewItem/itemID/13384 (accessed December 19, 2006).

7. Vladimir Simonov, "Russians Understand Putin Better than the West," *RIA Novosti,* March 15, 2004.

8. A December 2006 poll, conducted for Leonid Brezhnev's centennial, showed that what Russia most wants now is a new Brezhnev, whose years of leadership first were disdained as the "era of stagnation," and now are nostalgically recalled as a "golden era of stagnation" ("Leonid Brezhnev and His Era," FOM: Public Opinion Foundation, December 19, 2006; english.fom.ru/highlights/1353 .html [accessed December 19, 2006]). Brezhnev (together with Stalin) is seen as the most popular leader in Russian history, who gave "justice and stability" to the nation. Putin too fits this mold of firmness and seriousness, which ensures stability and a strong state.

9. *The Bronze Horseman* (1833), a poetic drama about the poor clerk Yevgeny and the Saint Petersburg flood of 1824, is considered one of Pushkin's finest works.

10. This quote is from Pushkin's *The Tale of Czar Saltan* (1831), which is as well known to all Russian children as *Dr. Seuss* and *Where the Wild Things Are* are to their American counterparts.

11. Cf. chapter 1, note 32.

12. Cf. chapter 2, note 16.

13. Dostoevsky's *The Idiot* (1868), which glorifies tragedy by preaching that every advocate of evil requires a champion of good, was the first in a series of state cultural projects for television adaptations of authors of historic importance. *The Idiot*'s hero Prince Myshkin, with his suffering and forgiveness, offers a potent message today as it revives for the people the notion of social equilibrium, destroyed by the unruly capitalism of the 1990s.

14. Pyotr Chaadaev, *Polnoe sobranie sochinenii i izbrannye pisma*, vol. 1 (Moscow, 1991), 527.

15. Ibid., 326.

16. Yelena Prudnikova, *Stalin: Vtoroe ubiistvo* (Saint Petersburg: Neva, 2003), 9.

17. *Kto vinovat?* (*Who Is to Blame?*) (1841–46) is a novel by Alexander Herzen. *Chto delat?* (*What Is to Be Done?*) (1863) is a novel by Nikolai Chernyshevsky. The latter's character and works then became the subject of Fyodor Godunov-Cherdyntsev's analysis in *The Gift*.

18. See, for example, *PF*, 274; Boyd, *Vladimir Nabokov: The American Years*, 476.

Chapter 1. Imagining Nabokov

1. Abram Tertz (Andrei Sinyavsky), *Strolls with Pushkin* (New Haven, Conn.: Yale University Press, 1993), 55.

2. Tertz, *A Voice from the Chorus*, 247.

3. Ibid.

4. Weber, *The Protestant Ethic*, 60.

5. Ibid.

6. Rodion Romanovich Raskolnikov is the miserable and megalomaniacal hero of Dostoevsky's novel *Crime and Punishment* (1866) who murders a hated old lady, a pawnbroker, with an ax—one of the best-known crimes in Russian literature.

7. Isaiah Berlin, "Political Ideas in the Twentieth Century," in Isaiah Berlin, *Four Essays on Liberty* (Oxford: Oxford University Press, 1969), 17.

8. In his essay "Nikolay Gogol: The Overcoat" (54–61) in *Lectures on Russian Literature* Nabokov, of course, writes about Gogol, not himself, and the exact quote reads as follows: "I can only place my hand on my heart and affirm that I have not imagined Gogol."

9. Cf. Boyd, *Vladimir Nabokov: The American Years,* 421–23, 459–60.

10. *SO,* I#19, 192.

11. Ibid., I#21, 197.

12. Ibid., I#15, 160–61.

13. Ibid., I#8, 109.

14. Cf. chapter 2, note 24.

15. *SO,* I#13, 149.

16. *RLSK,* 60.

17. *SM,* 106.

18. *Ada,* 541.

19. Ibid., 543.

20. *SO,* I#19, 186.

21. *Ada,* 541.

22. *SM,* 9–10.

23. Ibid., 242.

24. Ibid., 215.

25. *Pnin,* 387.

26. Ibid., 367.

27. Vladimir Nabokov, "Softest of Tongues," quoted in Beaujour, *Alien Tongues,* 95.

28. Michael Wood, *The Magician's Doubts: Nabokov and the Risks of Fiction* (Princeton, N.J.: Princeton University Press, 1995), 96.

29. Ibid., 94.

30. Ibid.

31. Cf. chapter 2, note 15.

32. The arc, circle, ring, round curve (Chaadaev: "we move forward not in a linear but a curving, circular fashion," cf. Prologue, note 15) is a shape of choice for the Russians. This circle, seen as a sign of harmonious autonomy in relation to the rest of the world, reflects the enclosed nature of Russian culture and the Russian land. Moscow's geography is circular: the Garden Ring defines the city contours above ground, the Circle metro line defines them underground. In literature too roundness is an important criterion of talent: "The figure of the circle with its intricate family including all sorts of ellipses and lemniscates best corresponds to Pushkin's spirit, in particular to his method of hunting down his heroes by tossing the line of fate, like a lasso, which manages in the course of the story to roll itself into a pretzel, a noose. . . . The roundest writer in Russian literature, Pushkin everywhere exhibits a tendency to close the circle, whether it be the contour of events or the sharp outline of a stanza strung like ring-shaped rolls into rhymed gardens" (Tertz, *Strolls with Pushkin*, 66).

   The most recent example of this "round uniqueness" is Alexander Sokurov's film *Russian Ark* (*Russkii Kovcheg*, 2000), which addresses issues of Russian national identity and the uneasy relationship between Russia and the West. Filmed in one shot, the movie describes an arc, ending in the same spot it started its dreamlike journey through the spaces of the hermetically enclosed ark of Russian culture, the Hermitage Museum in Saint Petersburg. Thus, in Sokurov's view, the Russian *kovcheg*—Russian art—is not only the savior of Russia and the rest of the world from the West, i.e. from debasing American culture, but in its form it also replicates a traditional Russian circle. In another "circular motion," Sokurov's address "Sailing the Russian Ark to the New World" (2002) reverts to a very familiar theme from the Russian past—the country's messianic destiny: "And tell [the Americans] that the time has come again for people to build arks and that there must be no delay, and that the Russians have already built their Ark, but not just for themselves—they will take all

with them, they will save all . . ."; www.landmarktheatres.com/
Stories/ark_frame.html (accessed September 24, 2006).

33. Cf. chapter 3, note 1.

34. Both bad weather and poor harvests were a routine explanation for
    food shortages and famine during Soviet times.

35. This opening sentence of *Ada, or Ardor* is a play on the famous be-
    ginning of Leo Tolstoy's *Anna Karenina* (1873–87), "Vse schastlivye
    semyi pokhozhi odna na druguyu, kazhdaya neschastlivaya semya
    neschastna po-svoemu" ("All happy families are more or less alike,
    each unhappy family is unhappy in its own way").

36. Axenty Ivanovich Poprishchin is an insane minor civil servant in
    Gogol's *Diary of a Madman* (1835), Konstantin Dmitrievich Levin
    is a shy philosopher-landowner in Tolstoy's *Anna Karenina*, Nikolai
    Alekseevich Ivanov is a character from Chekhov's eponymous play
    Ivanov (1887–89).

37. *Lolita*, 183.

38. *BS*, 175.

39. Ibid., xviii.

40. This monument was installed in the Montreux Palace lobby for
    Nabokov's centennial, just a few months before I visited with him. It
    was the work of Alexander and Phillip Rukavishnikov, father and
    son from a long-lasting dynasty of sculptors, which started at the
    turn of the last century with the sculptor Mitrofan Rukavishnikov,
    a distant relative of Vladimir Nabokov's family.

41. Cf. Introduction, note 33, and chapter 2, note 16.

42. In *The Stone Guest*, the longest and the most complicated of four
    short plays that comprise Pushkin's collection *Malenkie tragedii* (*Lit-
    tle Tragedies*, 1830), Pushkin retells the story of Don Juan and the
    Commendatore.

43. Footnoting this interview, Nabokov used his customary charade
    manner to explain: "Research has failed to confirm the existence of
    this alleged 'Dutch Master,' whose name is only an alphabetical step
    away from being a significant anagram, a poor relations to Quilty's
    anagrammic mistress, 'Vivian Darkbloom'" (*SO*, I#6, 73). It would

be reasonable to assume that Van Bock was meant as one of the anagrams of Nabokov's own name, such as Vivian Damor-Block, author of the "Index" in *Ada, or Ardor*. In an interview with the *New York Times Book Review* (February 17, 1968) Nabokov was asked about his social circle. In responding, "Mrs. Vivian Badlook," he supposedly meant Véra, his more social alter ego (*SO*, I#8, 110).

Chapter 2. On the Way to the Author

1. In his novel *What Is to Be Done?*, one of the most tendentious and radical works of Russian literature, Chernyshevsky based his ideal of cooperative socialism as well as his critique of capitalist individualism on his theory of "rational egoism." A better society could be achieved by maximizing the pleasure of the largest number of people, i.e. providing them with happiness in the workplace, which would benefit the society as a whole. The enlightened individuals, or "rational egoists," such as Rakhmetov—one of the novel's main characters, "an extraordinary man,"—aspired to maximize society's interests at the expense of their own personal pleasures. Through abstinence, sobriety, strength, high morality, the efficacy of every step, every action, even every morsel of food consumed, they were to assist humanity in becoming generally happy: "They [extreme measures] are necessary. We demand complete enjoyment of life for all people. Therefore, in our own lives we must demonstrate that we demand this not to satisfy our own passions, not for ourselves alone, but for man in general. We must show that we're speaking according to principles and not passions, according to convictions and not personal desires." Nikolai Chernyshevsky, *What Is to Be Done?* (Ithaca, N.Y.: Cornell University Press, 1989), 280–81.

2. Pechorin is usually very much adored by high school girls, who, when they've grown up and encounter these kinds of men in real life, turn their literary hearts to Bashmachkin and Makar Devushkin, a character from Dostoevsky's *Poor Folk* (1844). Although an indispensable character in Russian literature, Pechorin, as well as Onegin, is seen as an "otritsatelnyi geroi" (negative hero): while

possessing certain individualistic features of Western, Byronic (if not Weberian) man, they are both destroyers, not creators.

3. Andrei Shtoltz—Oblomov's best friend and his antithesis, a Russian of German descent. Shtoltz, businesslike and entrepreneurial, tries to convince Oblomov to change his lazy lifestyle.

4. Petya Trofimov is the "eternal student" of Chekhov's "comedy" *The Cherry Orchard* (1903).

5. Vladimir Nabokov, *Lolita,* in Vladimir Nabokov, *Sobranie sochinenii amerikanskogo perioda v pyati tomakh* (Saint Petersburg: Simpozium, 1999), 2:386.

6. Tertz, *A Voice from the Chorus,* 327–28.

7. Weber, *The Protestant Ethic,* 114.

8. Cf. Introduction, note 32.

9. Tertz, *A Voice from the Chorus,* 138.

10. Ibid., 212.

11. Pyotr Chaadaev, *Filosofskie pisma,* in P. S. Taranov, *Filosofskaya aforistika* (Moscow: Ostozhe, 1996), 553.

12. Tertz, *A Voice from the Chorus,* 248.

13. Joseph Brodsky (1940–96) was awarded the Nobel Prize for Literature in 1987 for his Russian-language poetry. He was exiled from the Soviet Union in 1972. After moving to the United States, Brodsky continued to write most of his poems in Russian and his prose in English.

14. Not always, however. He didn't mind, in fact, insisted on its other type—the literal rendering of poetry in a language of translation. See Vladimir Nabokov, trans., *Eugene Onegin: A Novel in Verse,* by Aleksandr Pushkin, 2 vols. (Princeton, N.J.: Princeton University Press, 1990), 1:viii.

15. Nikolai Gogol, *Dead Souls* (Penguin, 1961), 258–59. *Dead Souls* famously starts with a wheel, and ends with a troika carriage flight, thus serving as a model for a "koltsevaya" (circular) narrative composition, cherished by many writers as a typically Russian literary form.

16. This and the next quote in this paragraph are from Tertz, *Strolls with Pushkin,* 71. Baron Georges-Charles d'Anthès was a French exile in

Saint Petersburg as of 1834. Pushkin dueled with him in 1837 protecting the honor of his wife, imperial court society beauty Nataliya Nikolaevna Goncharova.

17. Stacy Schiff, *Véra {Mrs. Vladimir Nabokov}* (New York: Random House, 1999). Also see *SO*, I#3, 29; I#6, 77; I#10, 125; I#21, 198.

18. Mikhail Bulgakov, *The Master and Margarita* (New York: Vintage International, 1996), 247. Bulgakov was working on this novel from 1926 until the end of his life. The book was first published in 1967 and quickly became an artistic, satirical, and profound "bible" of Soviet life, providing us with razor-sharp one-liners of wisdom or humor. Almost every Soviet person of a certain generation could quote excerpts from the novel by heart.

19. Similar answers were published in a 1964 *Playboy* interview (*SO*, I#3, 26).

20. Tertz, *A Voice from the Chorus*, 272–73.

21. Ibid., 40.

22. The epigraph is from the Russian *Drugie berega*. In *Speak, Memory* the same quote reads as follows, "In a first-rate work of fiction the real clash is not between the characters but between the author and the world" (*SM*, 227–28). In *Strong Opinions*, however, Nabokov corrects the English version to resemble the Russian one: "I believe I said 'between the author and the reader,' not 'the world,' which would be a meaningless formula, since a creative artist makes his own world of worlds. He clashes with readerdom because he is his own ideal reader and those other readers are so very often mere lip-moving ghosts and amnesiacs" (*SO*, I#18, 183).

23. Wood, *The Magician's Doubts*, 101.

24. *Conclusive Evidence* was the original title of Nabokov's memoirs, first published in 1951, and republished in 1966 as *Speak, Memory*.

25. Tertz, *Strolls with Pushkin*, 71–72. "The Shot" (1830) and "The Queen of Spades" (1834) are novellas where, as in *The Stone Guest* (cf. chapter 1, note 42), at the end death becomes a punishment for the daring characters.

26. Nabokov, "Lance," in *The Portable Nabokov*, 203.

27. Vladimir Korolenko, "Paradox" (1894). Korolenko was a nineteenth-century liberal journalist and short story writer.

28. Witold Gombrowicz, "A Reply to Cioran," in *Altogether Elsewhere: Writers on Exile,* ed. Marc Robinson (San Diego, Calif.: Harcourt Brace, 1996), 155.

29. For a detailed account of why "Germany had always seemed to us [Russians] a country where *poshlust* [*sic*], instead of being mocked, was one of the essential parts of the national spirit, habits, traditions, and general atmosphere," see *NG,* 64.

30. The image of a lone chess king provided the original title for the novel *Bend Sinister,* then for the unfinished novel *Solus Rex* (1940), the precursor to *Pale Fire.* We find this image in many novels, and Nabokov repeatedly mentioned it in interviews.

31. Wood, *The Magician's Doubts,* 99.

32. Ibid.

33. The kindly nobleman extracts a two-inch splinter from the boy's back because "he was constantly being brought people who were wounded, maimed, even infirm" (*G,* 113). But this doesn't change the fact that the master treats *all* his property—horse, dog, rifle, boy—with the same benevolent owner's care.

34. Cf. chapter 3, note 86.

35. Max Weber, "The Protestant Sects and the Spirit of Capitalism," in Weber, *The Protestant Ethic,* 146.

36. See Alexis de Tocqueville, *Democracy in America* (New York: Harper Perennial, 1988), 699–702.

37. Weber, "The Protestant Sects," 135.

Chapter 3. Poet, Genius, and Hero

1. Pushkin, "Pora, moi drug, pora, pokoya serdtse prosit" ("It's time, my friend, it's time") (1834). For more on the *Dolya-Volya* comparison see Tertz, *Strolls with Pushkin,* 72–73.

2. I. A. Brodsky, *Bolshaya kniga intervyu,* ed. V. Polukhina (Moscow: Zakharov, 2000), 547.

3. Tertz, *A Voice from the Chorus,* 8.

4. Michael Wood, "Broken Dates: Proust, Nabokov, and Modern Times," in *Nabokov's World*, vol. 2: *Reading Nabokov*, ed. Jane Grayson, Arnold McMillin, and Priscilla Meyer (New York: Palgrave, 2002), 165.

5. Tertz, *Strolls with Pushkin*, 72.

6. Tertz, *A Voice from the Chorus*, 45.

7. Russian: Pushkin, "Exegi Monumentum" (1836): "Ya pamyatnik sebe vozdvig nerukotvornyi, / K nemu ne zarastet narodnaya tropa, / Voznessya vyshe ya glavouyu nepokornoi / Aleksandriiskogo stolpa. / Net, ves ya ne umru—dusha v zavetnoi lire / Moi prakh perezhivet i tleniya ubezhit—/ I slaven budu ya, dokol v podlunnom mire / Zhiv budet khot odin piit." In Nabokov's English translation these stanzas read as follows: "No hands have wrought my monument; no weeds / will hide the nation's footpath to its site. / Czar Alexander's column it exceeds / in splendid insubmissive height. / Not all of me is dust. Within my song, / safe from the worm, my spirit will survive, / and my sublunar / fame will dwell as long / as there is one last bard alive." (ruslit.virtualave.net/pushkin/emengl.html)

8. Ibid.

9. Tertz, *Strolls with Pushkin*, 65, 70–71.

10. Weber, *The Protestant Ethic*, 60.

11. Ibid., 160.

12. "Mozart and Salieri" is one of the *Little Tragedies*.

13. Vladislav Khodasevich, "O Sirine," in *Klassik bez retushi: Literaturnyi mir o tvorchestve Vladimira Nabokova*, ed. N. G. Melnikov and O. A. Korostelev (Moscow: Novoe literaturnoe obozrenie, 2000), 222.

14. Khodasevich, "Zashchita Luzhina," in *Klassik bez retushi*, 67.

15. "Pismo k N. N. Berberovoi, Mart 1939," in Vladislav Khodasevich, *Sobranie sochinenii v chetyrekh tomakh* (Moscow: Soglasie, 1997), 4:528.

16. Alexander Panchenko, "Tsivilizatsia levshi," *Nevskoe Vremya*, 5 March 1993.

17. Wood, *The Magician's Doubts*, 17.

18. See Edmund Wilson, *Upstate: Records and Recollections of Northern New York* (New York: Farrar, Straus and Giroux, 1970), 154–62.

19. Tocqueville, *Democracy in America,* 436.

20. To be fair, there are instances when Nabokov does mention other writers with recognition and respect: "If I am allowed to display my very special and very subjective admiration for Pushkin, Browning, Krylov, Chateaubriand, Griboedov, Senancour, Kuchelbecker, Keats, Hodasevich, to name only a few of those I praise, . . . I should also be allowed to bolster and circumscribe that praise by pointing out to the reader my favorite bogeys and shams in the hall of false fame" (*SO,* A#4, 266). He should be allowed that, no doubt. The problem with Nabokov, though, is that his positive attitudes drown in the sea of his negative ones.

21. Private conversation with Michael Wood, Princeton, N.J., April 22, 2003.

22. Tertz, *Strolls with Pushkin,* 65.

23. "The Covetous Knight" is one of Pushkin's *Little Tragedies.* It tells the story of a miserly baron who'd rather die than share his riches. In his indispensable *History of Russian Literature* (New York: Vintage Books, 1958) Prince D. S. Mirsky calls this minidrama "one of the greatest and grandest studies of the miser" (100).

24. See Elaine Feinstein, *Pushkin: A Biography* (Hopewell, N.J.: Ecco Press, 1998), 152–53, 158.

25. Quoted in Viktor Erofeev, "Russkaya proza Vladimira Nabokova," in Nabokov, *Sobranie sochinenii v chetyrekh tomakh* (Moscow: Pravda, 1990), 1:5. In response to this comment of Nabokov's, I would argue that this is not "despite," but "because of political hardships." Poetry does require an emotional upheaval, a drama, a collapse, which the twentieth century provided for Russia in good measure.

26. Mikhail Zoshchenko (1894–1958) was the most popular writer of satirical stories about Soviet life, which are told from the point of view of a semiliterate pretentious philistine. Ilya Ilf (1897–1937) and Yevgeny Petrov (1903–42) were the authors of two very famous Soviet satirical novels, *Twelve Chairs* (1928) and *The Golden Calf* (1931), that deal with the times of Lenin's New Economic Policy

and Stalin's first Five Year Plan. The fame of Yuri Olesha (1899–1960) comes from his short novel *Envy* (1927), which tackles the conflict between a new Soviet man and an ineffectual dreamer of the past. The work of these writers contains, although mostly disguised as humor, a profound critique of the Soviet order.

27. Ivanov and the three sisters, Olga, Masha and Irina, are characters of Chekhov's plays *Ivanov* and *Three Sisters* (1901), respectively. Ivan Petrovich Voinitsky (*Uncle Vanya*, 1899) is the character of the eponymous tragic comedy that is thematically preoccupied with what could be perceived as a "wasted life." The tragedy in Chekhov's dramas is the tragedy of continuance—events happen, but life doesn't change. In *Three Sisters*, for example, the sisters—Irina, to be precise—desperately want leave their dreary provincial life and move to Moscow. However, the play's famous refrain, "To Moscow! To Moscow! To Moscow!" never results in this very move.

28. Russians, who by 1991 en masse had gotten profoundly tired of their amorphous soulfulness, usually used the word "normalno" when they referred to the "Western" lifestyle in comparison with their own. In Russian this particular concept implies "to be civilized," "Western, not Asian," "live like people live," "the way life should be," i.e. livable, without sweeping revolutions and crises, dramatic outbursts, and romantic suffering and death.

29. Osip Mandelshtam (1891–1938), from a Saint Petersburg Jewish family, attended that city's liberal Tenishev School like Vladimir Nabokov, and then studied in Heidelberg. Upon returning to Petersburg in 1911, together with Akhmatova he became well known as the leader of Acmeism, a poetic school that sought to establish Russian poetry as a continuous tradition in world culture. At first Mandelshtam accepted the 1917 Bolshevik Revolution as a liberating force, but soon after realized that Stalinist communism was just a new name for the traditions of Russian despotism. In the 1930s Mandelshtam was exiled for his poetry to Cherdyn and Voronezh, and in 1937 he was sentenced to hard labor in the Siberian gulag where he died the following year.

30. Boris Pasternak (1890–1960), best known in the West for his novel *Doctor Zhivago* and the scandal that the book's publication abroad produced in Khrushchev's Soviet Union, was one of the leading twentieth-century Russian poets.

31. Zhivago derives from the word *zhivoi* (alive) while Mertvago comes from *mertvyi* (dead).

32. See Boyd, *Vladimir Nabokov: The American Years*, 423.

33. This and the next quote in this paragraph are from Osip Mandelshtam, "Pyotr Chaadaev" (1914–15) in Osip Mandelshtam, *Sobranie sochinenii v dvukh tomakh* (Moscow: Khudozhestvennaya literatura, 1990), 2:155–56. Incidentally, Saint Petersburg is a case in point.

34. Osip Mandelshtam, "Stone" ("Kamen"), in *Complete Poetry of Osip E. Mandelstam* (Albany, N.Y.: SUNY Press, 1973), 32.

35. Cf. above, note 18.

36. Mandelshtam, "To Ariosto" ("Ariost") (1935) in *Complete Poetry*, 219.

37. Mandelshtam, "Poet o sebe" (1928), in *Sobranie sochinenii*, 2:310.

38. Osip Mandelshtam, "The Noise of Time" (1923), in *The Prose of Osip Mandelstam*, ed. Clarence Brown (Princeton, N.J.: Princeton University Press, 1965), 122.

39. Kondraty Ryleev (1795–1826) was a minor Russian poet best known for his Byronic narrative poems. One of the leaders of the 1825 Decembrist Revolt (cf. below, note 72), he was hanged after its suppression.

40. Mandelshtam, "I was never anyone's contemporary" ("Net, nikogda, nichei ya ne byl sovremennik") (1924), in *Complete Poetry*, 139–40.

41. Mandelshtam, "Armenian words are wildcats" ("Dikaya koshka—armyanskaya rech") (1930), ibid., 185.

42. Mandelshtam, "Falling is how it feels to be afraid" ("Padenie—neizmennyi sputnik strakha, i samyi strakh est chuvstvo pustoty") (1912), ibid., 48–49.

43. Tertz, *A Voice from the Chorus*, 174.

44. Osip Mandelstam, "Fourth Prose," in *The Noise of Time: The Prose of Osip Mandelstam* (San Francisco: North Point Press, 1986), 183, 186.

45. Mandelshtam, "On Pope Benedict XV's Encyclical" ("ENCY-CLYCA") (1914) in *Complete Poetry*, 74.

46. Mandelshtam, "And I walk out of space" ("Vosmistishiya: 'I ya vykhozhu iz prostranstva'") (1933–35), "No comparisons: everyone alive is incomparable" ("Ne sravnivai: Zhivushchii nesravnim") (1937), "Poem on an Unknown Soldier" ("Stikhi o neizvestnom soldate") (1937), in *Complete Poetry*, 227, 272–73.

47. Mandelshtam, "Pyotr Chaadaev," 154–55.

48. Tertz, *A Voice from the Chorus*, 248.

49. Mandelshtam, "O prirode slova" ("On the Nature of the Word") (1922), in *Sobranie sochinenii*, 2:186.

50. Mandelshtam, "Fourth Prose," 179.

51. Both Delalande and John Shade (*Pale Fire*) are Nabokov's fictional inventions.

52. Mandelshtam, "I'm not dead, I'm not alone" ("Eshche ne umer ty, eshche ty ne odin") (1937) in *Complete Poetry*, 267.

53. Mandelshtam, "Fourth Prose," 181–82.

54. Ibid.

55. Mandelshtam, "January 1, 1924" (1924, 1937) in *Complete Poetry*, 137–38.

56. This and the following quote in this paragraph are from Mandelshtam, "Fourth Prose," 189, 186.

57. Mandelshtam, "We live, not feeling the ground under our feet" ("My zhivem, pod soboyu ne chuya strany") (1933), in *Complete Poetry*, 228.

58. S. S. Averintsev, "Sudba i vest Osipa Mandelshtama," in Mandelshtam, *Sobranie sochinenii*, 1:42.

59. Mandelshtam, "Rome" (1937), in *Complete Poetry*, 287.

60. Mandelshtam, "The Egyptian Stamp," in *The Noise of Time*, 161–62.

61. Mandelshtam, "Fourth Prose," 181.

62. Vladimir Nabokov, *Tyrants Destroyed and Other Stories* (New York: Penguin, 1981), 41.

63. Cf. above, note 56. The English translation of this poem in *Complete Poetry* is incorrect. In Russian Mandelshtam's line reads as

follows: "Chto ni kazn u nego, to malina i shirokaya grud osetina," meaning "Each execution is a joy for him, with his broad Ossetian chest." "Malina" in Russian doesn't only mean "raspberry," but is also a slang word for "joy," "good time," "easy life."

64. Abram Tertz, *Mysli vrasplokh,* in *Sobranie sochinenii v dvukh tomakh* (Moscow: SP Start, 1992), 1:333.

65. Victor Shklovsky, "Literature without a Plot: Rozanov," in Shklovsky, *Theory of Prose,* 190.

66. Karlinsky, "Nabokov and Chekhov," 14, 15. Cf. below, note 68.

67. Varya is a shy and romantic character in *The Cherry Orchard*; Dimitry Ionych Startsev is a successful and dreadfully boring provincial doctor in the story "Ionych," written in 1898; Belikov, an intimidating teacher who religiously follows all rules and regulations, is a character in another story, "A Man in a Box" ("Chelovek v futlyare"), also written in 1898.

68. In his article "Nabokov and Chekhov: The Lesser Russian Tradition," Simon Karlinsky has brilliantly examined the legacy of Chekhov's "biological humanitarianism" in Nabokov's work (cf. Introduction, note 35). Karlinsky opposes the work of Chekhov and Nabokov, medical doctor and biologist respectively, to the more common Russian literary tradition of "ideological humanitarianism" represented by Gogol, Dostoevsky, and others. In my opinion, however, Chekhov, like Nabokov after him, was a natural stage in the evolutionary development of all Russian literature, its step towards rationalization, not just as Karlinsky claims, to the "lesser Russian tradition of objectivity and precision" (14). Slowly, in its own mode of evolution, by revolutionary leaps and tremors, for several centuries now Russian culture has been moving in the direction of pragmatism and Westernism— from "human" to "humane," i.e. from personal humanism (*chelovechnost,* derived from *chelovecheskii,* human)—at times so overcharged that it becomes communal ideology—to biological, rational, individualistic humanitarianism (*gumannost*).

69. Cf. Schiff, *Véra,* 322–23; *SO,* I#13, 146.

70. Schiff, *Véra,* 325.

71. Dostoevsky, a known gambler himself, wrote a novel titled *The Gambler* (1867). Chernyshevsky, in creating the "new man" Rakhmetov in *What Is to Be Done?* used the experience of his own ascetic life.

72. On December 14, 1825, a group of officers led a regiment of soldiers to Senate Square in Saint Petersburg in demand for political reforms. The revolt of the "Decembrists" (many were Pushkin's friends) was severely suppressed: some of the participants were executed; others were exiled to Siberia.

73. Pushkin, "Vo glubine sibirskikh rud" (1827): "Vo glubine sibirskikh rud, khranite gordoe terpenie / Ne propadet Vash skorbnyi trud i dum vysokoe stremlenie" ("In far Siberia's deepest soil, / Preserve your proud, unflagging patience; / They won't be lost—your bitter toil, / And striving, lofty meditations"). The next stanza quoted in the text is from the same Pushkin poem. Translated by Rachel Douglas; www.schillerinstitute.org/transl/ trans_pushkin#vo-glubine (accessed December 5, 2006).

74. Cf. above, note 68.

75. Quoted in Victor Erofeev, "From Vladimir, with Style," *New York Times Book Review,* October 1, 1989; www.nytimes.com/books/ 99/04/18/specials/nabokov-letters.html (accessed May 10, 2005).

76. Vladimir Nabokov, "K kn. S. M. Kachurinu," in Nabokov, *Sobranie sochinenii russkogo perioda v pyati tomakh* (Saint Petersburg: Simpozium, 2000), 5:428–31.

77. Ibid., 748—49.

78. A daring suggestion: the same impulse could also inform his survivor's guilt, revealed in his nervously repetitive jibe at the blameless if imaginary Kachurin and in his displeasure with real political sufferers (Sinyavsky-Tertz or even Pasternak) who dared to face up to the regime.

79. Nabokov being Nabokov, however, immediately covers up all traces of his humanity. The scene following this conversation on Hunter Street is the bizarre tussle on Grimm Street at Quilty's Pavor Manor. The spectacular Humbert-Quilty chase through the keyless enfilade of rooms helps Nabokov, the masquerader, to disguise his

authorial intention of kindness. His trick is to mesmerize us (and obediently we are mesmerized) with this Hollywoodesque affair. No wonder he once mentioned that in Stanley Kubrick's cinematic version of *Lolita* "the killing of Quilty is a masterpiece" (*SO*, I#3, 21). In the book it's equally, if not more, theatrical, deceptive, and splendidly unreal, with references to plays and movie scripts, a "formless tussle on the part of two literati" (*Lolita*, 299). He must have calculated that the blinding brilliancy of this scene will make us forget what he just did—allowed beauty to merge with *poshlost* in a miracle of kindness and forgiveness. I could almost hear his voice, "You thought 'honey' meant something important. Wrong! Whatever you thought it meant, I didn't mean it. Quilty's and Humbert's tragic-comic scuffle is the episode you should concentrate on. It is of spectacular importance in *Lolita*." Sure it is—it safely conceals Nabokov's humanity in many mocking reflections.

80. Both quotes in this paragraph are from Dmitri Merezhkovsky, "Gogol and the Devil," in *Gogol from the Twentieth Century: Eleven Essays*, ed. Robert A. Maguire (Princeton, N.J.: Princeton University Press, 1974), 76–77.

81. Russian: F. M. Dostoevsky, *Bratya Karamazovy*, in *Sobranie sochinenii v semi tomakh* (Moscow: Leksika, 1994), 6:327. English: Fyodor Dostoevsky, *The Brothers Karamazov* (New York: Bantam, 1970), 359.

82. Michael Wood, "The American Nabokov," *The Nabokovian* 38 (Spring 1997): 30.

83. Fyodor Dostoevsky, *Devils*, trans. Michael R. Katz (Oxford: Oxford University Press, 1992), 742.

84. What makes the juxtaposition of Chekhov and Kafka possible is that Chekhov is not, as Karlinsky claims, an exponent of a "lesser," biological tradition in Russian literature, but a consistent follower of its "humanitarian" one. His works show how by the 1900s Russian ideological literature had reached an impasse of societal hopelessness, thus coinciding with the individual hopelessness of Western modernism as represented by a Prague resident of Jewish ancestry

writing in German. Kafka and Chekhov are two constituent parts of a single phenomenon—Western and Eastern (European) representatives of the nascent pragmatism of the twentieth century.

85. Cf. Introduction, notes 12, 15.

86. Lyubov Andreevna Ranevskaya is an eccentric and selfish estate owner in *The Cherry Orchard*. Leonid Andreevich Gaev is her impractical and wordy brother.

87. See above, note 68.

EPILOGUE. NABOKOV AS THE PUSHKIN OF

THE TWENTY-FIRST CENTURY

1. Tertz, *Strolls with Pushkin*, 79.

2. Cf. Introduction, note 33.

3. Tertz, *Mysli vrasplokh*, 321.

4. Vladimir Ilyich Lenin, "Pamyati Gertsena" ("In Memory of Herzen") (1912).

5. Cf. Chapter 3, note 7. In Russian this stanza from Pushkin's "Exegi Monumentum" reads as follows: "I dolgo budu tem lyubezen ya narodu, chto chuvstva dobrye v nem liroi probuzhdal. / Chto v svoi zhestokii vek vosslavil ya svobodu / I milost k padshim prizyval." In Nabokov's translation this stanza reads as follows: "And to the people long shall I be dear / Because kind feelings did my lyre extol, / Invoking freedom in an age of fear, / And mercy for the broken soul."

6. Andrei Bely (1880–1934) is best known for his novel of the Symbolist period, *Petersburg* (1916), which Nabokov hailed as "one of the three or four greatest novels of our time." (Quoted in Scammell, "The Servile Path," 58.)

7. According to Prince Mirsky's *History of Russian Literature* (195–96), Turgenev's most famous novel, *Fathers and Sons* (1862), along with its militantly materialistic and nihilist hero Bazarov, was in a way a response to criticism that in *On the Eve* Turgenev had failed to give Russia its own hero, instead choosing a Bulgarian when he wanted a respectable man of action.

8. The early poems of Sergei Yesenin (1895–1925) were inspired by folklore, but his work became increasingly solitary and dramatic toward the end of his life. Alexander Blok (1880–1922), who is sometimes dubbed a twentieth-century Pushkin, is credited together with Andrei Bely with the creation of Russian Symbolism during the "Silver Age" of Russian literature (the fin de siècle). His poetry influenced Anna Akhmatova, Marina Tsvetaeva, and Boris Pasternak, as well as Vladimir Nabokov.

9. Marina Tsvetaeva, "Est schastlivtsy i schastlivitsy" (1935) ("There are happy women and happy men"). Marina Tsvetaeva (1892–1941), together with Akhmatova, Mandelshtam, and Pasternak, is considered one of the greatest twentieth-century Russian poets.

10. Tertz, *Strolls with Pushkin,* 76.

11. Pushkin, "Svobody seyatel pustynnyi" (1823).

12. Cf. chapter 2, note 1. In *The Gift* Godunov-Cherdyntsev, a modern "rational egoist," writes of his ill-fated predecessor, "Chernyshevski's ethical structures are in their own way an attempt to construct the same old 'perpetual motion' machine, where matter moves other matter. We would very much like this to revolve: egoism-altruism-egoism-altruism . . . but the wheel stops from friction. What to do? Live, read, think. What to do? Work at one's own development in order to achieve the aim of life, which is happiness. What to do? (But Chernyshevski's own fate changed the businesslike question to an ironic exclamation)" (*G*, 282).

THE END

1. Khodasevich, "O Sirine," 220.

2. The last few years have indeed experienced a Salieri renaissance, a vindication from untrue gossip that plunged the eighteenth-century composer into musical history as Mozart's murderer. Considering it unfair that Salieri's fine operas were thrust into oblivion, the Teatro alla Scala in Milan restaged his 1778 opera *Europa Riconosciuta* (*Europe Revealed*) for its grand reopening in December 2004. The performance became an act of rehabilitation for Salieri's reputation.

Today some of the greatest Italian opera singers are performing his arias. The critics praise him, and recordings of his works are in high demand, certainly in Europe. The soprano Cecilia Bartoli recorded a selection of Salieri's pieces in 2003 to promote what she has called a forgotten and talented composer. Riccardo Muti, La Scala's music director, for example, claims that the score of *Europa Riconosciuta* shows moments of brilliance that in certain places rivals portions of Mozart's *The Magic Flute*. See Jason Horowitz, "A Renaissance of Sorts for Antonio Salieri," *New York Times,* January 5, 2005.

Envoi

1. This note is a clarification for Russian readers, who would surely question the validity of seeing a monument as a sign of true greatness. The Soviet Union was well known for erecting statues to such arbitrary cases as Andrei Zhdanov (1896–1948), the high Soviet official responsible for ideology (in 1948 he even got a city named after him), infamous for prosecuting such, much worthier, cases as Anna Akhmatova and Mikhail Zoshchenko. Russians would also doubt that once erected, a monument has a firm guarantee of remaining in its place—the USSR was equally known for destroying monuments for political reasons, or replacing some artistic, i.e. not "politically correct" enough, statues with more ideologically sound ones. For example, Nikolai Andreev's 1909 figure of Gogol seated in contemplation on Moscow's Prechistensky Boulevard was in 1952 replaced by another statue done by Nikolai Tomsky. This Stalin-ordered Gogol standing on the boulevard, now renamed Gogolevsky in his honor, was an optimistic Socialist Realist, with the inscription at his feet, "To the great artist in words, Nikolai Vasilievich Gogol, from the Government of the Soviet Union."

    In Soviet Russia public monuments did, indeed, become symbols of personal forgetting—not because they were slices of universal memory, but because whatever officialdom wanted us to remember the private memory was resentfully trying to purge. There a stone wasn't a step toward our common humanity—Russian evolution was repeatedly achieved by revolutions that always insisted on destroying the past in order to enter the future. Besides, Russia, particularly in its Soviet twentieth-century incarnation as an enclosed country, wasn't too keen on sharing anything with the rest of the world.

The future that is in peace with the past—i.e. the one in which monuments get erected and remain standing on the basis of merit not ideology—has a better chance to last in a linear, evolutionary, sensible, rational, even if at times prosaic, world—the world which Nabokov spent his life creating for us.

2. Since 2004 Nabokov has had to share his "treeless" park across the Palace with two bronze jazz musicians—Ray Charles and B. B. King, living legends of the Montreux Jazz Festival. The writer, who declared in his lifetime that "I loathe jungle music" (*SO*, I#9, 117), must forever witness his two neighbors playing the piano and the guitar. Fate has a sense of humor.

Select Bibliography

WORKS BY VLADIMIR NABOKOV IN ENGLISH

Ada, or Ardor. New York: Vintage International, 1990.

Bend Sinister. New York: Vintage International, 1990.

The Defense. New York: Vintage International, 1990.

Eugene Onegin: A Novel in Verse, by Alexander Pushkin. Translated from the Russian, with a commentary, by Vladimir Nabokov. 2 vols. Princeton, N.J.: Princeton University Press, 1990.

The Gift. New York: Vintage International, 1991.

Glory. New York: McGraw-Hill, 1971.

Invitation to a Beheading. New York: Vintage International, 1989.

Lectures on Literature. San Diego, Calif.: Harcourt Brace, 1980.

Lectures on Russian Literature. San Diego, Calif,: Harcourt Brace, 1981.

Lolita. New York: Vintage International, 1989.

Nikolai Gogol. New York: New Directions, 1961.

Pale Fire. New York: Vintage International, 1989.

Pnin, in *The Portable Nabokov.*

The Portable Nabokov. Edited by Page Stegner. New York: Penguin, 1978.

The Real Life of Sebastian Knight. New York: Vintage International, 1992.

Speak, Memory: An Autobiography Revisited. New York: Alfred A. Knopf, 1999.

The Stories of Vladimir Nabokov. New York: Vintage International, 1995.

Strong Opinions. New York: Vintage International, 1990.

Tyrants Destroyed and Other Stories. New York: Penguin, 1981.

WORKS ON VLADIMIR NABOKOV IN ENGLISH

Alexandrov, Vladimir E. *Nabokov's Otherworld.* Princeton, N.J.: Princeton University Press, 1991.

————, ed. *The Garland Companion to Vladimir Nabokov.* New York: Garland, 1995.

Appel, Alfred Jr. and Charles Newman, eds. *Nabokov: Criticism, Reminiscences, Translations and Tributes.* London: Weidenfeld and Nicolson, 1970.

Beaujour, Elizabeth Klosty. *Alien Tongues: Bilingual Russian Writers of the "First" Emigration.* Ithaca, N.Y.: Cornell University Press, 1989.

Boyd, Brian. *Vladimir Nabokov: The Russian Years.* Princeton, N.J.: Princeton University Press, 1990.

————. *Vladimir Nabokov: The American Years.* Princeton, N.J.: Princeton University Press, 1991.

————. "Nabokov and Humor." *The Nabokovian* 38 (Spring 1997), 38–43.

————. *Nabokov's Pale Fire: The Magic of Artistic Discovery.* Princeton, N.J.: Princeton University Press, 2001.

Chances, Ellen. "Čexov, Nabokov, and the Box: Making a Case for Belikov and Lužin." *Russian Language Journal* 140 (1987): 135–41.

Connolly, Julian W., ed. *Nabokov and His Fiction: New Perspectives.* Cambridge, UK: Cambridge University Press, 1999.

Field, Andrew. *Nabokov: His Life in Part.* New York: Penguin, 1977.

Grayson, Jane, Arnold McMillin, and Priscilla Meyer, eds. *Nabokov's World,* vol. 1: *The Shape of Nabokov's World;* vol. 2: *Reading Nabokov.* New York: Palgrave, 2002.

Hyde, G. M. *Vladimir Nabokov: America's Russian Novelist.* London: Marion Boyars, 1977.

Pichova, Hana. *The Art of Memory in Exile: Vladimir Nabokov and Milan Kundera.* Carbondale: Southern Illinois University Press, 2002.

Scammell, Michael. "The Servile Path (Translating Vladimir Nabokov by Epistle)." *Harper's Magazine* 302 (May 2001): 52–60.

Schiff, Stacy. *Véra {Mrs. Vladimir Nabokov}.* New York: Random House, 1999.

Wood, Michael. *The Magician's Doubts: Nabokov and the Risks of Fiction.* Princeton, N.J.: Princeton University Press, 1995.

———. "The American Nabokov." *The Nabokovian* 38 (Spring 1997): 26–30.

GENERAL REFERENCES IN ENGLISH

Berlin, Isaiah. *Four Essays on Liberty.* Oxford: Oxford University Press, 1969.

———. *Russian Thinkers.* London: Hogarth Press, 1978.

Blinov, Artur. "Report: Energeticheskii dialog na fone politicheskogo krizisa." *Nezavisimaya Gazeta,* March 1, 2006.

Brzezinski, Zbigniew K. *The Grand Chessboard: American Primacy and Its Geostrategic Imperatives.* New York: Basic Books, 1998.

Bulgakov, Mikhail. *The Master and Margarita.* New York: Vintage International, 1996.

Chernyshevsky, Nikolai. *What Is to Be Done?* Translated by Michael R. Katz, annotated by William G. Wagner. Ithaca, N.Y.: Cornell University Press, 1989.

Dostoevsky, Fyodor. *The Diary of a Writer.* New York: George Braziller, 1954.

———. *The Brothers Karamazov.* Translated by Andrew H. MacAndrew with introductory essay by Konstantin Mochulsky. New York: Bantam, 1970.

———. *Devils.* Translated and edited by Michael R. Katz. Oxford: Oxford University Press, 1992.

Eckel, Mike. "Putin Calls Collapse of Soviet Union 'Catastrophe.'" Associated Press, April 25, 2005.

Feinstein, Elaine. *Pushkin: A Biography.* Hopewell, N.J.: Ecco Press, 1998.

Gogol, Nikolai. *Dead Souls.* Translated with an introduction by David Magarshack. London: Penguin, 1961.

————. *Diary of a Madman and Other Stories.* Translated with introduction by Ronald Wilks. London: Penguin, 1972.

Hall, Edward T. *Beyond Culture.* New York: Anchor Press, 1976.

Hall, E. T. and M. R. Hall, *Understanding Cultural Differences.* Yarmouth, Maine: Intercultural Press, 1990.

Harrison, Lawrence E. and Samuel P. Huntington, eds. *Culture Matters: How Values Shape Human Progress.* New York: Basic Books, 2000.

Hellbeck, Jochen. *Revolution on My Mind: Writing a Diary under Stalin.* Cambridge, Mass.: Harvard University Press, 2006.

Maguire, Robert A., ed. *Gogol from the Twentieth Century: Eleven Essays.* Princeton, N.J.: Princeton University Press, 1974.

Mandelstam, Osip. *The Prose of Osip Mandelstam.* Edited and translated by Clarence Brown. Princeton, N.J.: Princeton University Press, 1965.

————. *Complete Poetry of Osip E. Mandelstam.* Translated by Burton Raffel and Alla Burago, with introduction and notes by Sidney Monas. Albany, N.Y.: SUNY Press, 1973.

————. *The Noise of Time: The Prose of Osip Mandelstam.* Translated with critical essays by Clarence Brown. San Francisco: North Point Press, 1986.

Mirsky, D. S. *History of Russian Literature.* New York: Vintage, 1958.

Nepomnyashchy, Catharine Theimer. *Abram Tertz and the Poetics of Crime.* New Haven, Conn.: Yale University Press, 1995.

Niemeir, Susanne, Charles P. Campbell, and Rene Dirven, eds. *The Cultural Context in Business Communication.* Philadelphia: John Benjamin, 1998.

Ostrovsky, Arkady. "Gazprom Acts as Lever in Putin's Power Play." *Financial Times,* March 13, 2006.

Pipes, Richard. "Flight From Freedom: What Russians Think and Want." *Foreign Affairs* 83, no. 3 (May/June 2004): 9–15.

Putin, Vladimir. Opening Address at the Meeting with G8 Finance Ministers. Kremlin.ru. February 11, 2006.

Robinson, Marc, ed. *Altogether Elsewhere: Writers on Exile.* San Diego, Calif.: Harcourt Brace, 1996.

Shklovsky, Victor. *Theory of Prose.* Translated by Benjamin Sher with an introduction by Gerald L. Bruns. Elmwood Park, Ill.: Dalkey Archive Press, 1991.

Simonov, Vladimir. "Russians Understand Putin Better than the West." RIA Novosti, March 15, 2004.

Sinyavsky, Andrei. *Soviet Civilization: A Cultural History.* Translated by Joanne Turnbull with the assistance of Nikolai Formozov. New York: Little, Brown–Arcade, 1990.

Smith, Adam. *An Inquiry into the Nature and Causes of the Wealth of Nations.* Edited by Edwin Cannan, with a new preface by George J. Stigler. Vol. 4. Chicago: University of Chicago Press, 1976.

Tertz, Abram (Andrei Sinyavsky). *A Voice from the Chorus.* Translated from the Russian by Kyril Fitzlyon and Max Hayward. New York: Farrar, Straus and Giroux, 1976.

———. *Strolls with Pushkin.* Translated by Catharine Theimer Nepomnyashchy and Slava I. Yastremski. New Haven, Conn.: Yale University Press, 1993.

Tocqueville, Alexis de. *Democracy in America.* Edited by J. P. Mayer, translated by George Lawrence. New York: Harper Perennial, 1988.

Weber, Max. *The Protestant Ethic and the Spirit of Capitalism.* New introduction and translation by Stephen Kalberg. Los Angeles: Roxbury, 2002.

Wilson, Edmund. *Upstate: Records and Recollections of Northern New York.* New York: Farrar, Straus and Giroux, 1970.

Works by Vladimir Nabokov in Russian

Drugie berega. In Nabokov, *Sobranie sochinenii v chetyrekh tomakh,* vol. 4. Moscow: Parvda, 1990.

Nabokov o Nabokove i prochem. Edited and compiled by Nikolai Melnikov. Moscow: Nezavisimaya Gazeta, 2002.

Select Bibliography

Sobranie sochinenii v chetyrekh tomakh. Moscow: Pravda, 1990.

Sobranie sochinenii amerikanskogo perioda v pyati tomakh. Saint Petersburg: Simpozium, 1999–2000.

Sobranie sochinenii russkogo perioda v pyati tomakh. Saint Petersburg: Simpozium, 2000.

Ten russkoi vetki: Stikhotvoreniya, prosa, vospominaniya. Moscow: Eksmo, 2000.

WORKS ON VLADIMIR NABOKOV IN RUSSIAN

Averin, B., M. Malikova, and A. Dolinin, eds. *V. V. Nabokov: Pro et Contra: Antologiya.* Saint Petersburg: Russkii Khristianskii Gumanitarnii Institut, 1997.

Brodsky, I. A. *Bolshaya kniga intervyu.* Edited by V. Polukhina. Moscow: Zakharov, 2000.

Melnikov, N. G. and O. A. Korostelev, *Klassik bez retushi: Literaturnyi mir o tvorchestve Vladimira Nabokova.* Moscow: Novoe literaturnoe obozrenie, 2000.

Lyuksemburg, A. and Rakhimkulova, G. *Magistr igry Vivian Van Bok: Igra slov v proze Vladimira Nabokova v svete teorii kalambura.* Rostov on Don: Izdatelstvo instituta massovykh kommunikatsii, 1996.

Nosik, Boris. *Mir i Dar Nabokova: Pervaya russkaya biografiya pisatelya.* Moscow: Penaty, 1995.

Shulman, Mikhail. *Nabokov, Pisatel. Manifest.* Moscow: Nezavisimaya Gazeta, 1998.

Stark, V. P., ed. *A. S. Pushkin i V. V. Nabokov: Sbornik dokladov mezhdunarodnoi konferentsii, 15–18 aprelya 1999 goda.* Saint Petersburg: Dorn, 1999.

GENERAL REFERENCES IN RUSSIAN

Aksakov, Konstantin. *Sobranie sochinenii v dvukh tomakh.* Moscow, 1911.

Blok, Alexander. *Gorod moi: Stikhi o Peterburge-Petrograde.* Leningrad: Lenizdat, 1957.

Chaadaev, Pyotr. *Polnoe sobranie sochinenii i izbrannye pisma.* Vol. 1. Moscow, 1991.

Chekhov, A. P. *Chaika: Piesy 1880–1904.* Moscow: AST-Folio, 1999.

———. *Dama s sobachkoi: Rasskazy 1887–1899.* Moscow: AST-Folio, 1999.

Chkhartishvili, Grigory. "Pokhvala ravnodushiyu." *Znamya—Plus* (1997–98): 182–89.

Dostoevsky, F. M. *Besy.* In *Sobranie sochinenii v semi tomakh,* vol. 4. Moscow: Leksika, 1994.

———. *Bratya Karamazovy.* In *Sobranie sochinenii v semi tomakh,* vols. 6–7. Moscow: Leksika, 1994.

Khodasevich, Vladislav. *Sobranie sochinenii v chetyrekh tomakh.* Moscow: Soglasie, 1997.

Mandelshtam, Osip. *Sobranie sochinenii v dvukh tomakh.* Moscow: Khudozhestvennaya literatura, 1990.

Maslin, M. A., ed. *Russkaya ideya.* Moscow: Respublika, 1992.

Prudnikova, Yelena. *Stalin: Vtoroe ubiistvo.* Saint Petersburg: Neva, 2003.

Pushkin, A. S. *Zolotoi tom: Sochineniya A. S. Pushkina v odnoi knige.* Moscow: Imidzh, 1993.

Shklovsky, Viktor. *Energiya zabluzhdeniya: Kniga o suyzhete.* In *Izbrannoe v dvukh tomakh,* vol. 2. Moscow: Khudozhestvennaya literatura, 1983.

Sinyavsky, Andrei. *Ivan-Durak: Ocherk russkoi narodnoi very.* Moscow: Agraf, 2001.

Skalkovsky, K., ed. *Russkie o Russkikh: Mneniya Russkikh o samikh sebe* (1904). Saint Petersburg: Petro-Rif, 1992.

Taranov, P. S. *Filosofskaya aforistika.* Moscow: Ostozhe, 1996.

Tertz, Abram (Andrei Sinyavsky). *Sobranie sochinenii v dvukh tomakh.* Moscow: SP Start, 1992.

Tsvetaeva, Marina. *Stikhotvoreniya i poemy.* Leningrad: Sovetskii pisatel, 1979.